OUR COMMUNITY

Dealing with Conflict in Our Congregation

Susan M. Lang

Augsburg Fortress
Minneapolis

OUR COMMUNITY
Dealing with Conflict in Our Congregation

Developed in cooperation with the Division for Congregational Ministries of the Evangelical Lutheran Church in America, Michael R. Rothaar, project manager.

Scripture quotations are from New Revised Standard Version Bible, copyright © 1989 Division of Christian Education of the National Council of the Churches of Christ in the United States of America. Used by permission.

Series overview: David P. Mayer, Michael R. Rothaar
Editors: Laurie J. Hanson, James Satter

Cover design and series logo: Marti Naughton
Text design: James Satter
Cover photograph: Gordon Gray, FRPS

About the cover image: The centerpiece of the Resurrection Window in First Lisburn Presbyterian Church, Northern Ireland, was created by stained glass artist James Watson, Belfast, from fragments of church windows destroyed by a car bomb in 1981 and restored after a second bomb in 1989. The window symbolizes new life in Christ, which transforms darkness to light, hatred to love, despair to hope, and death to life. The members of First Lisburn Presbyterian have lived out this promise through new initiatives for community service, reconciliation, and peace-making.

ISBN 0-8066-4411-7

The paper used in this publication meets the minimum requirements of American National Standard for Information Sciences—Permanence of Paper for Printed Library Materials, ANSI Z329.48-1984.

Manufactured in the U.S.A.

06   05   04   03   02   1   2   3   4   5   6   7   8   9   10

✠ Contents

Series Overview

Welcome to the Congregational Leader Series, and welcome to the journey of discovering God's future for you and your congregation. Your congregation's mission and ministry are given to you by God. We sometimes refer to "our church," but it is always Christ's church. We are at best its stewards or caretakers, not its owners. As we plan, organize, and lead, we strive toward excellence in everything we do to reflect the glory and grace of God, who has entered human life to redeem us.

As a congregational leader, you may be asking, "What is our mission? How should we structure things? How can we plan for the future and where will the resources come from?" The Congregational Leader Series provides resources for effective planning and leadership development. Each book includes biblical and theological foundations for planning and leadership development, and practical information to use in building on your congregation's strengths.

We are first of all called to be faithful to God's word and will. Exploring the Bible enables us to discern what God's plan is for us as individuals and as a congregation. Ignoring or minimizing the centrality of God in our deliberations risks not only failure but also our faith. In the words of the psalmist, "Unless the LORD builds the house, those who build it labor in vain"(Psalm 127:1).

Why should we engage in congregational planning and leadership development? When the congregation is at its best, these activities aid us in fulfilling our mission to the world: reaching out with the gospel of Jesus Christ. Faithful planning for mission mirrors God's activity in the world, from creating and covenant-making to gathering and renewing the church. When congregations fail to plan, they risk dissipating the resources they have been given by God and begin falling away from all that God has intended for them.

In short, faithful planning and leadership development engage the congregation and all its members in the creative work of God. Continually analyzing and shaping our vision, mission, ministry, and context allows us to ask, "What is God calling our congregation to be?" Working to develop and support leaders enables us to ask, "How has God gifted each of us for ministry?"

We begin with prayer

As congregational leaders, we always begin our endeavors with prayer. Discerning God's will for us is a task that requires that we be in communication with God. Unfortunately, we often come up with new ideas and programs—and then pray that God will bless them! That order needs to be reversed. Our prayers should precede our plans, helping us discern God's call to us.

In his few years of public ministry, Jesus accomplished a tremendous amount of healing, teaching, and service for others. However, his ministry did not begin until after he had spent an extended period of time in the wilderness reflecting on his call and God's purpose for his life. Following that retreat, virtually every moment of his life's story was punctuated with prayer and ultimately concluded with his supplications in Gethsemane and on the cross.

Paul wrote to the Thessalonians, "Rejoice always, pray without ceasing, give thanks in all circumstances; for this is the will of God in Christ Jesus for you" (1 Thessalonians 5:16-18). These words were meant for us—congregational leaders anxious to get on with things that need to be done. Notice how Paul places *prayer* between *rejoice* and *thanks* in this verse. Prayer is not simply another task to be done nor an obligation to be met. It is a gift of God to be celebrated and used with joy and thanksgiving. It is meant to permeate our lives. As leaders, we are seeking to construct God's will in our communities. God invites us to build with gladness and to make prayer the mortar between every brick we lay.

As congregational leaders, we always begin our endeavors with prayer.

We build from strength

Most leadership resources begin with the assumption that there is a problem to be solved. In the midst of the real problems that surround us, however, our task as congregational leaders is to identify the strengths, giftedness, and blessings that God has given to us and the congregation. Our primary calling is not to be problem-solvers but to be asset-builders. Paul reminds us, "Let all things be done for building up" (1 Corinthians 14:26). This is not license to ignore problems, conflicts, or deficiencies. Rather, it is a call to view the brokenness around us in a new way.

Our primary calling is not to be problem-solvers but to be asset-builders.

Our role as Christian leaders is to attempt to look at our congregation, our fellow Christians, and ourselves, as God sees us. "This is my commandment, that you love one another as I have loved you" (John 15:12). Jesus did not blindly ignore the problems around him. Instead, he viewed those problems through a lens of love, appreciation, and forgiveness. We are called to build from strength, to construct our plans and visions from what God has given us. When we try to build from weakness and focus only on our problems, we compound both and ultimately fail.

First Church was located in a growing, well-to-do suburb, on a main thoroughfare, and in a beautiful new building. The members of First Church appeared to have everything going for them, and the congregation's future looked very bright.

The congregation, however, faced an ongoing problem with mortgage payments. This problem became so all-consuming that the congregation began to lose sight of its strengths, gifts, and mission for the future. The members of First Church had everything they needed to solve the problem of mortgage payments but they were unable to stop fixating on it. Soon, many other issues surfaced as everyone became a fault-finder.

Today there is no mortgage-payment problem because there is no First Church. The preoccupation with weakness and deficiency blinded the congregation to the reality of its gifts. This congregation died, not because of its problems but because of its perspective.

We must constantly ask ourselves and others, "Where is God at work here? What gifts have we received for ministry in this place?" Focusing only on what we don't have breeds jealousy, competition, hopelessness, and lost vision. Focusing on our gifts gives birth to joy, affirmation, and hope.

We won't find quick fixes

We live in a culture obsessed with quick fixes and mesmerized by the notion that there is a prescription for every ailment and accident. But things keep falling apart. People get sick. Programs fail. Committees don't function. Plans backfire. And goals aren't met. The list of mistakes, failures, misfires, and flops grows and grows. In his letter to the Romans, Paul reminds us that "all have sinned and fall short of the glory of God"(Romans 3:23). Paul says this not to weigh us down with despair, but instead to remind us that our salvation comes from God and not ourselves.

Faithful leaders have a deep respect for the reality of problems and obstacles. Things will always fall apart. That's why planning, assessing, goal-setting, leading, and visioning are ongoing processes, not quick fixes. As leaders, we need to know the nature of sin and publicly acknowledge its pervasiveness. Then we can lead, not with unhealthy fatalism, but with honesty, humility, and a sense of humor.

We are all ministers

As Christians, everything we do and plan is communal. We cannot plan unilaterally or devise strategies in isolation. To be sure, each of us has received salvation individually through baptism, but at that moment, through the water and the Word, we were united with the body of Christ. Even the gifts that God has given each of us are meant for the common good of all God's people: "To each is given the manifestation of the Spirit for the common good" (1 Corinthians 12:7).

Each of us is a minister, whether pastor or lay person, and each of us is called to serve others.

In other words, each of us is a minister, whether pastor or lay person, and each of us is called to serve others. This is a radical departure from our culture's overwhelming emphasis on individual independence. The idea that we are all ministers and that as the church we minister as a community has tremendous implications for all of our planning and development efforts.

Leadership development is nothing more than equipping the members of the congregation so that they are strengthened for ministry: "The gifts he gave were that some would be apostles, some prophets, some evangelists, some pastors and teachers, to equip the saints for the work of ministry, for building up the body of Christ" (Ephesians 4:11-12). Paul would be appalled at the idea that a paid professional minister should carry out all of the ministry of the congregation or that only some people in the congregation are called to ministry.

Faithful planning and leadership development affirm that all of God's people are gifted and invited to participate in ministry. Identifying, embracing, and strengthening each other's gifts for common mission is a daunting task that never ends, but through that effort and in that journey we become what God intended: "But you are a chosen race, a royal priesthood, a holy nation, God's own people, in order that you may proclaim the mighty acts of him who called you out of darkness into his marvelous light" (1 Peter 2:9).

A model for understanding congregations

Congregations are extremely complex. Throughout the Congregational Leader Series, we invite you to look at your congregation through a particular model or set of lenses. This model helps us to understand why congregations are so complex, and it provides some important clues for the leadership skills and tasks that are needed.

A congregation resembles three different institutions at the same time: a *community of spiritual formation*, a *voluntary association*, and a *nonprofit organization*. This isn't a matter of size—the largest and smallest are alike in this. It isn't a matter of context—the model applies to both urban and rural settings. Each type of institution has different values and goals, which may even contradict each other. Each of these values and goals requires different things from leaders.

Communities of spiritual formation

A congregation is, in part, a community of spiritual formation. People come to such a community to join with others in growing closer to God. They seek to understand God's word and God's will for their life. They seek an experience of God's presence, a spiritual or emotional awareness of transcendence and love. They seek time for contemplation and prayer, and also time to work with others on tasks that extend God's love to others.

How are our congregations communities of spiritual formation? Much of congregational life centers on worship. We teach children and adults the practice of faith. The church provides support in Christ's name during times of crisis and need. We engage in visible and public activities, such as offering assistance to people who are homeless, or hungry, or survivors of abuse, as a way of both serving God and proclaiming God's mercy and justice.

The most important value in a community of spiritual formation is authenticity.

The most important value in a community of spiritual formation is authenticity. There is no room for pretense, no room for manipulation, and no room for power games. The goals we establish must be clearly directed to outcomes in people's spiritual lives. The fundamental question for self-evaluation is this: "How has our ministry brought people closer to God?"

Voluntary associations

Like any club or voluntary association, a congregation is a gathering of people who are similar to one another in specific ways, share a common purpose, and largely govern and finance their organization's existence and activities. In addition, people often find that belonging to a club is a way to make friends and social or business contacts, and enjoy meaningful leisure time activities. Some voluntary associations, such as Kiwanis or Lions clubs, have charitable purposes and sometimes seek support from people beyond their own membership. Some voluntary associations are focused on common interests or activities, such as gardening or providing youth athletic leagues.

Membership requirements may be strict or fluid, costs may be high or low, and commitments may be long or short, but they are spelled out rather clearly. A number of unwritten rules may serve to get people to conform to common values. Most voluntary associations would like to have more members, both to strengthen their organization and to expand the social benefits that come from a broader circle. But the new members usually are people who are very much like those who are already members.

The most important value in a voluntary association is effectiveness in helping people relate to one another.

The most important value in a voluntary association is effectiveness in helping people relate to one another. The goals are largely relational. There must be many opportunities for people to form relationships, especially with those with whom they have much in common. The association must operate in such a way that people all feel that their own values and hopes are being well served, usually through direct access to the decision-making process and ample opportunities for public dissent. People want and expect to be contacted regularly by both leaders and other members, and to feel that they are fully accepted as part of the group.

It is also important that there is a consensus—a shared vision—on what the association is and does. When conflict emerges, it must be negotiated and resolved. Because membership is voluntary, when there's conflict, or when they just don't feel part of the group anymore, people are usually quick to withhold their financial support or quit altogether.

Nonprofit organizations

As if it weren't complicated enough to be both a community of spiritual formation and a voluntary association, now consider that your congregation is also a nonprofit organization. It is a chartered or incorporated institution, recognized as a legal entity by the federal, state, and municipal government. A congregation can borrow and lend, sue and be sued. You as a congregation are accountable to society and responsible for following all applicable laws. Almost all congregations are property owners and employers. The congregation has formal operational procedures and documents (from your constitution to state laws) that dictate how you must make decisions and conduct your affairs. The usually unspoken but fundamental goal of a nonprofit organization is self-perpetuation, making sure that the institution will continue.

In this regard, congregations are similar to any business that offers services to the public. Being *nonprofit* simply means that the organization's assets can't be distributed to individuals or for purposes contrary to the charter. It doesn't mean that the congregation can't or shouldn't be run in a businesslike manner—or that it can't accumulate assets. The actual operation doesn't differ much from that of a profit-making business. In a nonprofit organization, the primary value is efficiency, or achieving the greatest results with the least possible expenditure of resources.

Another core value is continuity, with orderly systems that must be applied by anyone who carries out the organization's work. To reach financial goals, a nonprofit organization seeks voluntary contributions and often regularizes revenue through endowments and ancillary sources of income. Efforts are made to minimize costs without sacrificing quality. The organization also tries to build reserves to meet unanticipated circumstances and periodic needs (such as replacement of depreciating assets). Policies are in place to protect the staff and volunteers, and to ensure clear and mutually agreed upon expectations. There are clear lines of accountability and each person operates within a specified scope of decision-making.

In a nonprofit organization, the primary value is efficiency, or achieving the greatest results with the least possible expenditure of resources.

Planning in a nonprofit organization includes making the best use of property and facilities. The property is seldom an end in itself, but the goal of leadership is always to maximize its usefulness. Other organizational goals revolve around having a truly public presence, including marketing effectively, identifying the needs and wants of a particular group of people, developing a product or service that addresses those needs, and informing the target group of its desirability and availability. Nonprofit organizations must do this as surely and skillfully as those in the profit sector.

You may have heard that "you shouldn't be a manager, you should be a leader." This is unfortunate language, because management is part of leadership, and voluntary organizations need managers. How you analyze, organize, delegate, supervise, and evaluate the congregation's work is critical to its vitality.

Leadership

What does the word *leadership* really mean? Think of it as having three dimensions: *character*, *knowledge*, and *action*. *Character* permeates all three aspects of this model. Leaders have principles and try to live them out. In any of the three ways in which we're looking at congregations, leaders are honest, trustworthy, dedicated, caring, disciplined, and faithful to the core principles—and have many more virtues as well. Although everyone sins and fails, be clear that improvement is expected from all leaders.

It is not only character that counts. Leaders must also know things and do things. *Knowledge* and *action* can be developed. They can be learned in books and classes or from working with people who have expertise. Things we know from one part of our experience can be applied to other parts of our lives.

Applying the congregational model

The three-part model of congregations is helpful in exploring the different things that leaders must be, know, and do in a community of spiritual formation, in a voluntary association, and in a nonprofit organization.

Problems develop when the values, goals, and leadership styles appropriate to one part of the congregational model are mistakenly applied to one of the others. It is not wrong to value authentic spirituality, effective interpersonal relationships, and operational efficiency. There are times when each of these should be given the highest priority. Recognize that your congregation probably has emphasized one of these areas at the expense of the others, and plan your way to a better balance. Embrace the wonderful complexity of congregational life and ask God to move among us to change us and renew us and rededicate us to God's own purposes.

The Congregational Leader Series

This is one of several books in the Congregational Leader Series. The entire series seeks to build on the positive, basing your planning on assets rather than deficiencies, and to focus on outcomes, enabling your congregation to make a specific and definable difference in people's lives. The series has two sets: congregational planning and leadership development. Books in this series can be used in any order, so you can get started with those books that are most helpful for you and your congregation. The reproducible tools can be used with your council, committees, planning teams, leadership groups, and other members of the congregation. Visit www.augsburgfortress.org/CLS to download and customize these tools.

Faithful planning and leadership development take us on a journey, a pilgrimage, and an exploration of God's possibilities for you and your congregation. The Congregational Leader Series provides resources for your travels, as you seek God's will and guidance for you and your congregation.

This image of a cross indicates that further information on a topic appears in another book in the Congregational Leader Series.

Introduction

Conflict is inevitable, but combat is optional.

Max Lucado, *Let the Journey Begin*

A major bequest, changes in worship, the addition of a preschool to your church building - all these things and more can spark strong reactions in individuals and congregations.

Each of us approaches life with a set of values and personal needs. When something collides with those values and needs, we react. As leaders in the congregation, we should never forget Isaac Newton's law that every action has an equal and opposite reaction—and the bigger the action, the bigger the reaction. This phenomenon seems to apply to organizations as much as it applies to physics.

To add to this, a change that seems small to us may in fact be monumental to a person struggling with health or personal issues. It may be their proverbial last straw and their reaction could be more volatile than we expected. In this case, the conflict may not be about us but instead about the struggles the other person is undergoing. We can learn to deal with situations like this in Christian love and compassion. That's the start of a stronger community of faith.

As the Series Overview indicates, congregations are a complicated mix of communities of spiritual formation, voluntary associations, and nonprofit organizations. We can be sure in any decision-making process that different individuals will prioritize one aspect of congregational life over another. That's a recipe for conflict right there.

Gossip sessions and impromptu caucuses that develop in the church parking lot after worship or committee meetings are warning signs. When communication goes underground like this instead of staying above board, there is trouble brewing. It's inevitable.

You may be experiencing conflict in your congregation right now or you may see storm clouds looming on the horizon. Whether your congregation is in the early stages of conflict or in the heat of battle, it's never too late to deal with controversy. While the general rule is that there is less damage in tackling the problem in the early stages, there is still much to learn in advanced situations of conflict.

The Congregational Leader Series seeks to build from strength. That's a challenge for us when we are in conflict, for it's hard to see the strengths when we are lost in our weakness and our confusion. It is hard to see our unity as the people of God when we are obsessed with our differences.

As people of the resurrection, we have faith that God makes all things new. God can and will raise us from the ashes of our human pride and inadequacies. God gives us new life and new hope through Jesus Christ. Hold fast to that promise at all times and find strength in the one who loves and empowers us to serve in Jesus' name.

God makes all things new.

What this book can do

There are no easy answers for dealing with conflict in the congregation. In reality, conflict is part of change and renewal in both our personal lives and in our congregations. The entrance into new life is not a painless process. Neither is spiritual or communal growth.

Conflict will exist in the life of the congregation; we can't escape that. What we can escape, though, is the human tendency to deal with conflict by acting without thinking. By slowing down and looking at the nature of conflict from a variety of angles, we can develop new insights and operate from a position of strength.

Approaching all controversy from a biblical perspective will shed new light on the fear and darkness that encompasses us when we attempt to deal with troublesome situations. We are not alone. Immanuel, God with us, accompanies us on all journeys of life—especially those rocky roads and stormy nights.

How to use this book

Use this book on your own or in your congregation council to make sense of a past controversy, better understand a current situation, or build skills for dealing with conflict in a healthy manner. Your council and other groups or committees in the congregation might also use the material on developing more effective communication skills to enhance their group dynamics and prevent the unhealthy escalation of conflict.

If you use this book with a group, be sensitive to the fact that each individual is at his or her own place. Some people might not participate in a discussion or group process or see things the same way you do. Even small steps can be steps in the right direction. Don't undermine your efforts with expectations that are too high.

Overview of book

Chapter 1: Our Perceptions of Conflict—What is conflict and how does its presence affect us? Recognizing that all change involves conflict empowers us to think through how we deal with controversy. A "blueprint for change" can help us plan new directions in ministry and mission.

Where two or three are gathered, there is sure to be disagreement at some point.

Chapter 2: Who We Are as People of God—Conflict and disagreements are as old as time itself. Where two or three are gathered, there is sure to be disagreement at some point. You can bet on it. Chapter 2 looks at some biblical stories of conflict and what God says to us through those stories and events (including the biblical directive from Matthew 18 that is the basis for our communal life as the people of God).

This chapter also reviews major events in the lives of the current generations within our congregations. Recognizing that each generation has a different set of group experiences and values helps us to understand why there are often generational clashes in congregations.

Chapter 3: Family Systems and Congregational Dynamics—A congregation is made up of many diverse individuals and families who gather to worship and celebrate their unity in Jesus' name. Our home or family life can affect our interaction with the congregational family. Awareness that we can cause damage to the life of a congregation by carrying our dirty laundry into the pews helps us leave that dirty stuff at home.

Recognizing the ghosts of conflicts past in our personal and communal lives helps us control the influence they have over us now. If you can name it and claim it, it has less power over you. You operate from a position of strength.

Chapter 4: Community Conflict—Healthy conflict empowers vitality and growth in the Body of Christ while unhealthy conflict causes "dis-ease" and unrest. How do we learn to confront conflict while living with humor and forgiveness as guiding principles? How can we avoid blame games and grudges?

Chapter 5: Learning Life Skills—Communication, both verbal and non-verbal, is the basis for all interaction in life. This chapter discusses basic guidelines for communication and how to work with groups to enable better speaking and listening. What is really being said in some situations? The real issue isn't always found in what is first indicated, but sometimes in how things are said or done.

Chapter 6: Surviving the Storms—The boat is rocking, now what? When the seas of our congregational life toss us to and fro, we need tools to stay focused and navigate the storm. Some of the ingredients of conflict can cause us to lose focus and actually prolong the conflict. This happens especially with conflict that is aimed directly at us. But conflict can be depersonalized so that we can deal with it in a more rational manner and stay out of the line of fire when it's not aimed at us.

Building community trust begins at the level of the congregation council. Learning healthy decision making and sticking together when decisions are inevitably questioned are part of what it means to be an effective leader. So is the realization that the very act of leadership involves conflict. Stating clear goals and expectations, creating group covenants, and praying together will steady you when the boat is rocking.

Chapter 7: Storm Cleanup—Storms leave a lot of debris on the shore that must be removed. Conflict in congregations can damage the spirit and health of the congregation or it can create a new hope and vision for the future. The direction it takes depends on what we as congregational leaders do after the storm settles.

Conflict will drain the leaders of a congregation. Even if we present a calm exterior while under fire, chances are pretty high that the adrenaline is pumping and the blood pressure rising. After all, we're only human. Pastors and lay leaders need to care for themselves not only during a conflict, but immediately afterwards. Controversy takes its toll. We need to practice good stewardship of our body, mind, and spirit. We can't be strong leaders if our spirit is broken.

Chapter checklists

Individually or in a group, use the checklists at the end of each chapter to answer the following questions:

- What is going well in our congregation? Do we act in ways that are consistent with the basic values and principles involved in this chapter?
- Based on this chapter, does our congregation have any areas for improvement or important responsibilities that are not being carried out at this time?
- How can we celebrate what is going well? What are the next steps to be taken in any areas for improvement or change?

Conflict toolbox

This book provides you with reproducible tools to use in self-assessment and group exercises. These tools are located in the Conflict Toolbox at the back of the book.

1. Self-assessments

You must know yourself before you can deal effectively with controversy in the congregation. Use the self-assessment tools for personal reflection. Depending upon the trust level, these tools also

> Above all, remember that your number one "tool" in, during, and after conflict is prayer. It's hard to be angry at someone whose name you lift to God each day in prayer.

could be used in a group by filling them out individually and then sharing what you have learned in groups of two or three.

2. Group exercises

During conflict, there is a tendency to shut down communications. This is not healthy for any community or individual. The main intent of the group exercises is to promote communication between people.

Healthy conflict

We are all imperfect people—sinners in need of transformation and dependent upon the love of God. There is always the opportunity to grow in faith and in life skills for our spiritual journey. We can learn to prevent the unhealthy escalation of conflict. When we remember that we are in need of new understanding and growth and that God loves us all, then we're on the road to dealing with conflict in a constructive and healthy manner.

Chapter 1

Our Perceptions of Conflict

We have met the enemy and it is us.

Walter Kelly, *Pogo* comic strip

We often think of conflict as a monster, like a fire-breathing dragon that is out of control. When it rears its ugly head, it terrifies us. We are frightened that we will be consumed by it.

Defining the monster

Conflict is a force pulling in opposite directions. It can be creative or destructive. Often when we think of conflict within our congregations, we think of two groups playing "tug of war," each with its own agenda, pulling until one group is pulled to the other side.

If we alter our perceptions to think of conflict as a creative force in life, we might find that where conflict occurs, growth is possible. Rather than a case of horizontal "tug of war" with "us" versus "them," perhaps the tug in situations of conflict is vertical. Perhaps God is encouraging us to change and grow, inviting us into a deeper relationship of faith.

The goal is to keep conflict constructive and life-giving. As soon as conflict escalates into a destructive force ("us" versus "them") everyone suffers. Conflict also can escalate when we respond to God's gentle tug by becoming adamant in our humanity and refusing to accept God's love and gracious invitation.

Two common responses to conflict

When congregational conflict breaks out, there are often two immediate responses: denial and damage control.

Denial

Maybe we can get used to the dragon. You know it might make a nice house pet. It might not be so bad. Perhaps it really doesn't consume that much. This is the "let's pretend it's not there, we're supposed to love and accept everyone so let's just forget about it and move on" response.

But conflict ignored is just like an illness. Denial allows the illness to continue to eat at the body until the individual members begin to suffer. Eventually pain and discord follow. Denial doesn't make conflict go away. It just gives opportunity for deeper cellular damage to occur.

Denial doesn't make conflict go away.

Damage control

We've got to get the dragon out of here immediately! In this response, we think, "Let's get this thing over as soon as possible. We surely don't want any of the folks in the new members class to pick up on what's going on. They might decide to leave. Worse yet, we might lose some big contributors over this."

Damage control may prematurely end what is perceived as purely destructive. A "let's do the first thing that comes to mind" mentality takes over. When this type of *reactivity* reigns, creativity has no chance to thrive. That includes the creative influence of the Holy Spirit present in our communities of faith. It's sad indeed that fear can cause us to rush ahead and not listen to God's call to us as the people of God. But this happens every day. We get scared and we act before we think.

Clearly, neither denial or damage control is the best course of action when dealing with discord within the body of Christ. The problem with dealing with conflict in a congregation is that often our first course of action is not well thought out. There's little attempt to obtain group ownership. That's a formula for disaster.

Life is conflict

Many people see conflict as a purely negative force—one that should be avoided at all costs. But is it really? Or are we just afraid of the idea itself and the feelings that it elicits in us?

But there is another way to think of conflict. In many ways, life itself is conflict. From the moment we get up in the morning to the time we go back to sleep at night, we're faced with a multitude of decisions concerning how we live, eat, work, and play. There's often a pull in two or more directions as we decide how to spend each day. We weigh what we will do and, in effect, place ourselves in a state of emotional conflict.

Any decision involves conflict.

Any decision involves conflict. Do you attend a retreat to uplift and feed your faith life or do you finish up some paperwork that you should have completed last week, but couldn't get to because of some emergency? Does the congregation council spend money on the latest in audiovisuals for the sanctuary to update worship and perhaps attract the younger generation? Or should the money be kept in the bank because last year the congregation was financially in the red? Whose needs do we focus on in the life of the congregation—more activities for the youth, or more for the verbal and increasing senior population?

Change is conflict

One of the things we learn early in life is that change equals conflict. Likewise, any change, any growth in ministry, can result in negative comments and a chance for conflict. If you have tried to introduce a second worship service in a contemporary style to a congregation that has had one service for one group of people for the past 100 years, you know this.

The pace of our 21st-century life is exhausting for many people. Many struggle with busy schedules. Parents transport their kids to a wide variety of activities. Families seldom eat dinner together. Everyone is scattered. People often come to church feeling out of control. That hour in the pew may be an opportunity to seek the comfort of a familiar worship service. Because we generally feel out of control when something that is comfortable and familiar suddenly changes, a change in the congregation, especially in its worship life, can produce conflict.

Seeds of congregational conflict

While change is a major cause of conflict in congregations, it's not the only one. Seeds of conflict can include:

- unclear roles or expectations
- poor communication
- power plays
- differing values
- personal versus congregational agendas
- disagreements over space or other property issues
- unexpected congregational crises, such as natural disasters or vandalism
- congregational growth

What other seeds of conflict would you add to this list?

As leaders, changes in ourselves, our homes, our work, and the congregation can result in stress and conflict. Use the "Change, Conflict, and You" tool on pages 91-92 to look at the changes in your life and the conflict that may be involved in those changes.

The best offense: education

If you know an avid football fan, you've probably heard this phrase: "The best defense is a good offense." In this case, we're not talking about beating the other side, but merely being proactive. This means recognizing that whenever something changes in the life of a congregation, somebody's going to get upset or vocal. Dissent can be stirred up between those who propose a change and those who don't support it—because of the change itself or the way it is presented. The best "offense" or approach to change is basic: educate, educate, educate.

Jesus taught his disciples the meaning of the changes that were to occur for them and for all humankind. He spoke of his life, his death, and even his resurrection. While his followers exhibited confusion along the way at what Jesus really meant, it all came together for them when they saw him risen from the dead. Talk about radical change! God had just conquered death and turned things upside down.

Talk about radical change! God had just conquered death and turned things upside down.

Jesus had prepared his disciples for what he knew was to come. Once they understood that his death and resurrection had changed everyone, they were excited to go forth and share with the world the message of God's deep love for us.

As leaders, our goal in any change we make is to have congregational members react in a similar way, with a life-giving excitement that can't be contained. So let's get started!

A blueprint for change

Analyze perceived needs

Why change anything? Change in itself isn't always right or necessary. Is there a perceived need for growth and development, whether it be to seek new ways to attract potential members or change the look of the sanctuary?

Identify what you perceive the needs to be in any proposed change. Share these needs with your congregation council, committee, or other working group. Do these members of the congregation agree with the needs you have identified? They may see things from a slightly different perspective. That's okay. Dialogue is good and can help you clarify the needs of the congregation.

Once you have clarified the perceived needs, list your goals for making a change. Keep this list in front of you at all times. It's amazing how you, the council, or committee can forget the goals and get sidetracked when conflict occurs.

Share the goals with the congregation through newsletters, brief talks, congregational meetings, and mailings. The bigger the change, the more communication is critical as the possibility of conflict looms larger. Help people understand the goals involved in a change and give them a chance for feedback so that they feel included in the process.

Seek viable options

Don't limit yourself as you seek options to meet your goals. Seek the guidance of the Holy Spirit. Survey the congregation. Get feedback through special meetings or through questionnaires. If congregation members feel included in the decision process, they will have more ownership in the result. Broader ownership can mean less conflict.

Broader ownership can mean less conflict.

Decide with the appropriate group

Weigh all the options. How does each option meet your goals? Which is the best option? Pray about this as a group.

Is the change a decision for your committee, congregation council, congregation as a whole, or a combination of these? Your congregation's constitution can provide some guidance on this. Be sure there is ample discussion in the appropriate groups and that all people have adequate time to have their questions answered.

You can agree to disagree at meetings, but once a committee or council decision is made don't carry your dissatisfaction to others outside the meeting. This can undermine the authority of your committee, council, or pastor.

Educate the congregation

Go public with your decision. Anticipate questions and consider a question-and-answer format in your newsletter or bulletin. Make sure everyone knows when the change will occur and exactly what it means. If you are planning on changing the time of a worship service, be sure to tell people well in advance.

When questions arise, realize that a question is just a question, not an attack. If you are anxious about the reactions a change will produce, it's easy to forget that. Sometimes people want the opportunity to feel included in the process by asking questions and receiving a response.

Monitor and adapt

You may find that your change needs some fine-tuning. Be prepared for that. Make adjustments as necessary. Adjusting the plan doesn't mean that the first action was a failure, just that you are open to more ideas and the creative activity of the Holy Spirit in your presence.

The words *change* and *conflict* should not frighten us. Conflict is not the terrifying beast we often think it is. When we fight against God's vertical call to grow in faith and take it out on each other, things become dysfunctional. That's called sin. As the people of God, we are transformed through our baptism and given the gift of faith and the promise of a new life through Jesus Christ. That's a change worth telling the world about!

To offer people who were homebound or hospitalized the opportunity to participate in the Lord's Supper on a more regular basis, one congregation began to explore the option of training and appointing what they called "Lay Eucharist Ministers." Questions were raised. Options were explored. The congregation council studied the topic from a theological perspective and decided to proceed.

The education process began with a guest speaker during a worship service and frequent newsletter articles on the plans for implementation. People who were homebound were surveyed on whether they would accept communion from a Lay Eucharist Minister and most supported the proposal. The council then selected five members who were trained and appointed as Lay Eucharist Ministers. A commissioning service was held for them during a communion service.

The Lay Eucharist Ministers now make their visits the first Sunday of each month. This ministry has been received very favorably by people who are homebound or hospitalized and has been deeply meaningful to the Lay Eucharist Ministers themselves.

Your views of conflict

It's important for you as a leader in a congregation to be in touch with your perceptions of conflict so that you can be more focused during tough times. Does conflict frighten you? Do you feel out of control when faced with people who disagree with you? Do you always have to be right? Do you see conflict as purely negative? Do you see conflict as an opportunity to grow and explore new options for life and for ministry? Before you begin to help others work though tough situations, begin to explore questions such as these.

In *Discover Your Conflict Management Style*, Speed Leas discusses a variety of management styles for dealing with conflict. These styles include persuading, compelling, avoiding/accommodating, collaborating, negotiating, and supporting. How do you generally deal with conflict? The more you know about your perceptions of conflict and your preferred styles for addressing it, the stronger you will be as a leader.

How do you generally deal with conflict?

To think about

1. Think of a current or past conflict in your congregation. Write it as you see it, adjectives and all. This is for your eyes only, so be brutally honest.

2. Once you've completed the honest description of the conflict, sit back and review what you've written. Slowly. Thoughtfully. If you have to take a break because just thinking about the conflict has stirred up intense feelings in you, do that. This in itself says a lot. When you come back to your description of conflict, underline all the words that express feelings. What do you see? How strong are your feelings? What does this say about you and this particular conflict situation? If there is an absence of feelings in your description, are there issues you may be avoiding?

3. What would ease your feelings about this conflict?

What have you learned? Do you detect any growing edges within yourself—areas you need to work on, either in regard to the specific conflict you wrote down, or about conflict in general?

Journaling

Useful insights for leadership can be obtained by journaling your thoughts, feelings, and observations amid conflicts. Because it's so easy to get caught up in the heat of battle, the goal is to learn to stop and think during conflicts so that you can respond with less reactivity.

Seeing your thoughts about conflict on paper can be startling, but it can also put you more deeply in touch with what you are truly feeling. You can't change anyone else, but clearly identifying your feelings and perceptions can help you to change your own perceptions and the way you respond to others.

Personal hooks and hot spots

What are your personal hooks and hot spots as a leader? What issues elicit a strong reaction in you? Are you high church in your worship style? Does the innocent suggestion of a praise band visiting Sunday worship cause a rise in your temperature? Do you believe that everything must be done following a strict, proper procedure? Are you upset when it's not?

Take the "Hooks and Hot Spots" self-assessment on pages 93-94. Make a list of the issues that cause your blood to boil. It's important to know those areas that might pull you into a conflict. Pay attention to them. Are they issues really worth fighting for? Only you can decide.

Summary

- Conflict is not something to be feared or avoided.
- Conflict within a congregation should not be denied; it should be addressed in a healthy manner.
- Conflict is a sign of life. View it as God's pull to grow in faith, not as a tug-of-war between human factions.
- Education and inclusion of members of the congregation in any process of change will encourage a healthy process.
- Celebrate the Holy Spirit's creative activity in your congregation.
- Identify your perceptions of conflict in your congregation.

Chapter 2

Who We Are as People of God

One of Jesus' specialties is to make
somebodies out of nobodies.

Henrietta Mears

We think of the Bible as a story of God's love. Yet look closely and you'll see conflict everywhere—-nation fighting against nation, internal community struggles, people rebelling against God. The Bible really reads as the identity crisis of the people of God. Throughout the Bible, there is a lot of acting out and a lot of bloodshed.

Our identity as people of God has always been a struggle between who we are in the world and who God is calling us to be. As humans, we are conditioned by our environment. Our families and the world we live in play a critical part in our self-definition. Frequently that self-definition contradicts God's intent for us. We may feel guilt or shame so that we can't fathom God's love for us. Arrogance may keep us from caring. Whatever our self-definition is, we struggle with the meaning of our baptism and how to live as the people of God. This struggle can put us in conflict with God, each other, and the world.

Stories of conflict in the Bible

Israel: people rebel against God

God made the people of Israel a chosen people, but they were never satisfied. They always wanted more: more love, more proof that they were favored by God, more blessings. After God led them out of Egypt, where they had been slaves, they did nothing but complain. (See the book of Exodus in the Bible.) Their inward focus kept them from celebrating their newfound freedom. It prevented them from using their God-given creativity to solve their problems.

How is God
reaching out to
you, even amid
conflict?

Even though the Bible portrays the identity crisis of the people of God, it also is an epic story of a God who wants a relationship with the people. The people turn from God, but God continues to reach out to them.

When your community suffers from an identity crisis, God still desires a relationship with you. How is God reaching out to you, even amid conflict? What doors that were previously closed are opened during a conflict in your community? Look for them. They may be God's invitations to a new relationship and a new direction in ministry.

Jeremiah: a prophet battles God's call

The story of Jeremiah shows us that individuals also struggle with what God calls them to be. Being a prophet has never been easy. Who wants to tell people that in the eyes of God their lives are sinful and they will be punished? Jeremiah sure didn't. He struggled from day one with his call to prophesy. He didn't think he was up to the task.

When you read the book of Jeremiah, you can understand why he balked. The message Jeremiah is called to give the people is heavy-duty. The imagery is stark. The people of Israel are portrayed as a whore, prostituting herself with foreign idols. God is angry and plans judgment upon the people by making them captive to Babylon. It is a severe punishment for abandoning God.

Jeremiah is imprisoned. He has death threats made against him. He also struggles intensely with his call to serve God. He burns with passion for God's word, yet curses the day he was born (Jeremiah 20:7-18). But from the start, God promised to stand by Jeremiah throughout all his doubts and suffering (Jeremiah 1:19). God keeps that promise. Jeremiah is preserved and he lives to see the fulfillment of the grim prophesies.

Do you, as a congregational leader, ever feel like Jeremiah, struggling with God's call? How does God speak to you in the midst of your struggles? Listen for the voice of God speaking to you. Just as God supported Jeremiah, God also supports you in your struggles.

Corinth: a fractured community

Paul planted the seeds for the Christian church in Corinth, but he became angered by the divisions that ensued. There was fighting and competition over who was their spiritual leader, Paul or Apollos (1 Corinthians 3:1-23). There was sexual immorality (1 Corinthians 5:1-13). The Corinthians couldn't even go to the Lord's Supper without problems and arguments (1 Corinthians 11:17-33). The church at Corinth was one big dysfunctional community struggling to understand itself as Christian in a pagan world.

Paul gave guidance by metaphorically speaking of the church at Corinth as the body of Christ. To remain healthy, members must care for one another, respect each other, and, most importantly, love one another (1 Corinthians 12:1—13:13). They were not to engage in pagan rituals or fight among themselves.

The Corinthians' new identity was in Jesus Christ and in his death and resurrection. These events changed everything. As Christians, they were to live transformed by the power of the cross and God's love for us all.

When your community is engaged in internal struggles, reread Paul's words to Corinth, a fractured community. We are all members of the same body. Pain inflicted on one member hurts us all. How do you see this communal pain exhibited in the life of your congregation? How can you be an agent of healing in the midst of community struggle and pain?

Acts: the church confronts the world

The Holy Spirit empowers the disciples to preach on Pentecost and immediately they face the reaction of the world. Some people hear and

Just as God supported Jeremiah, God also supports you in your struggles.

believe. Others think the disciples are drunk (Acts 2:1-42). The religious and secular leaders who acted to put Jesus to death are shocked that a movement in his name lives on. They persecute the early church. Stephen is stoned (Acts 7:54-60). James is killed and Peter is arrested (Acts 12:1-5). Many were martyred for proclaiming the love of God for all people through Jesus' death and resurrection.

The church of Christ has always confronted an angry and violent world. In Acts, we see the early Church more clearly defining itself so that its witness in the world might be unified and unambiguous. The decision is made to carry the Christian message to the Gentiles. Circumcision is not necessary for conversion to the new faith as it was in the Hebrew tradition. A new path is forged.

When we as the church see ourselves in conflict with the world, what must we do? The example of Acts is one to keep in mind. Rely on the guidance of the Holy Spirit. Define who you are as the church of Christ in your community. Put your heart into your mission and maintain the focus.

Matthew 18: a model for reconciliation

In Matthew 18, Jesus gives us a model for reconciliation within his church:

> If another member of the church sins against you, go and point out the fault when the two of you are alone. If the member listens to you, you have regained that one. But if you are not listened to, take one or two others along with you so that every word may be confirmed by the evidence of two or three witnesses. If the member refuses to listen to them, tell it to the church; and if the offender refuses to listen even to the church, let such a one be to you as a Gentile and a tax collector.
>
> Matthew 18:15-17

Matthew 18 provides a clear directive for dealing with an offender in our midst:

- While we are to forgive, we are also to be humble like children (Matthew 18:1-5), not arrogant.
- We are not to be the cause for anyone to stumble. All stumbling blocks should be eliminated (Matthew 18:6-9).
- God desires no one to be a lost sheep (Matthew 18:10-14).
- If someone sins against you, speak with that person. If that doesn't work, involve a couple of trusted individuals who will witness the conversation. If that attempt still is not successful, go to the larger gathering of believers. The absolute last resort is to exclude the nonrepentant troublemaker (Matthew 18:15-20).
- When an offender repents, forgiveness is to be as boundless as God's forgiveness is for us (Matthew 18:21-22).
- Punishment occurs for the unforgiving (Matthew 18:23-35).

The ramifications of Matthew 18 can be hard to swallow. Our congregational life is centered on the forgiveness forged by Jesus' death on the cross. Yet there are times when conflict or perversity within our communities of faith require us to take a stand. We are called to love, but when sin is purposefully committed in our midst, it must be addressed. We deny Christ if we allow sin to grow like a cancer within his church. It may seem benign at first, but it wastes no time becoming malignant. Death of the body is imminent if sin is ignored. The treatment Jesus recommends is communication—open and loving communication.

We deny Christ if we allow sin to grow like a cancer within his church.

What issues do you see as being issues that come under the blanket of Matthew 18? How is the determination reached that an individual or group is causing purposeful and hurtful damage to the body of Christ? What would be your first action if faced with a Matthew 18 incident? Start with prayer for the individuals and for the guidance of the Holy Spirit as you proceed. To look further into the directive in Matthew 18, use the Bible study on page 95.

Misconduct

When we hear the word *misconduct* we generally think of a serious breach of ethics on the part of a pastor. Lay misconduct happens, too. People with access to church funds embezzle. Sexual abuse of children by ministry workers has been a recent hot topic in the church.

Whether you're a pastor or lay leader who discovers an alleged incident of clergy or lay misconduct, take appropriate action.

Congregations in the Evangelical Lutheran Church in America, are required to report allegations immediately to the bishop's office and follow their instructions. The bishop's office will be in contact with legal counsel. In cases of clergy misconduct, the pastor is not allowed to stay in the congregation.

Take a proactive stance to misconduct with actions like these:

- Establish a policy for all ministry workers, including the pastor, who engage in work with children.

- Check backgrounds and get references for those seeking positions in your congregation. Those with nothing to hide have nothing to fear.

- Make sure checks and balances are in place for individuals handling church funds.

Living what we preach

When the Matthew 18 directive works, a brother or sister who has sinned repents. This means ending the act of committing the sin, asking for forgiveness from all damaged parties, and agreeing on guidelines for future interactions. When this is done, as Christians, we are called to forgive. In forgiveness everyone acknowledges their pain and moves on. That means not constantly reliving the past and dredging it up in conversation.

Reconciliation in the body of Christ means a coming together where distance and pain once separated us. It is a solemn yet joyous occasion where we truly recognize our own sinfulness and the gift of forgiveness that we all receive through Jesus Christ.

When reconciliation occurs, consider a way to acknowledge and celebrate it. Prayer, Scripture reading, and a sharing of the peace between all parties is not only appropriate—it is a solid witness to our call as Christians to love one another. What other ways might you celebrate a true act of reconciliation in your community of faith?

Our place in history

Who we are as the people of God is first defined by God's story as it comes alive throughout history. The time period in which we were born and raised also contributes to our complex identity as human beings. Technology, family values, historical events, the economy, and entertainment have an influence in how we develop our view of the world. What we experienced growing up is not the same as what our parents or grandparents experienced.

There are substantial differences between a generation that grew up with only the radio as its main contact with the outside world and the generation that is Internet savvy. One is not better than the other, but we need to recognize that the vocabulary of our lives just isn't the same.

Awareness of our differences is the first step toward diffusing conflict. We run into predictable conflicts in the congregation when one generation has trouble communicating with another or members of one generational group don't understand or accept the life experience of another group. You're likely to encounter generational differences in issues of clothing, respect, finances, and priority of the church in family life. One way to short-circuit these differences is to acknowledge them, discuss them, and celebrate them. Remember that the body of Christ is made up of many members and we're not all the same age or from the same culture. We don't interpret things in the same way. That's the beauty of our diversity.

Awareness of our differences is the first step toward diffusing conflict.

Through the generations

A variety of categories have been proposed to define the current generations that coexist in our world today. The names of the categories vary and there is also some disagreement over the exact years when one generation begins and ends. In spite of this, a categorization of the generations can give us a framework for looking at living generations and the things they have encountered at different stages of their lives.

In the book *Generations: The History of America's Future, 1584 to 2069* (New York: William Morrow, 1991), William Strauss and Neil Howe categorize the generations in this way:

G.I.	1901–1924
Silent	1925–1942
Boomer	1943–1960
13th generation	1961–1981
Millennial	1982–200?

The G.I. generation lived through World War I and the Roaring Twenties. They saw Prohibition and the beginning of commercial radio broadcasts. Members of this generation often serve as builders and team players, working with an emphasis on getting the job done together. They fought in World War II and held democracy together against great odds.

The Silent generation grew up during the Great Depression or World War II, seeing the effects of the attack on Pearl Harbor and the end of Prohibition. This generation was born too late to serve in World War II. They were smallest generation in terms of numbers, and they generally married young. Men and women of this generation often are viewed as cautious in lifestyle and decisions.

The Boomers were born into a world of *Sputnik*, the Korean War, McCarthyism, and the entrance of TV into many homes. Boomers include Vietnam vets as well as war protesters. The size of this generation has always drawn much attention from marketers and advertisers. Boomers are seen as inward-focused, seeking personal enrichment and satisfaction. They place a high priority on individualism.

(Although Strauss and Howe place the Boomers between the years of 1943 and 1960, other researchers place this generation between 1946 and 1964.)

The 13th generation (sometimes called Generation X) grew up during the aftermath of the Cuban missile crisis, the Vietnam War, and Watergate. People of this generation often are viewed as more street-wise than other generations, as many were latchkey kids fending for themselves while parents were at work. There is a high education level among the 13th generation. Members of this group are not known for seeking affiliation. They, too, are individualistic.

Millennials were born into the world of the fall of the Berlin Wall, the Persian Gulf War, and the attack on the World Trade Center. The oldest were preschoolers when the *Challenger* exploded in 1986 and interest in space exploration waned. Millennials are growing up with the world at their fingertips, with personal computers in their homes and schools. They are highly valued and protected by parents and elders.

The impact of generational differences

So much has happened at such a rapid pace within the past 100 years. It's no wonder that different generations see things differently. How might these differences in our experiences surface in the life of our congregation?

Use the "Generational Values in Your Congregation" tool on pages 96-97 to facilitate group discussion and recognition of some of the historical factors and events that contribute to differences in the way generations view things. Discuss how the leaders in your congregation view issues. Are all the generations represented in the leadership of your congregation? Does one generation dominate your leadership? If so, what implications might that have on decisions?

As human beings, we are complex individuals who come together to worship a God who has given us a new identity through the cross of Jesus Christ. Learn to use your differences for creative means rather

How might these differences in our experiences surface in the life of our congregation?

than divisive means. As a Church we are stronger when we draw on the gifts and talents of all the members of the body of Christ.

Summary

- The people of God throughout history have struggled with the meaning of their identity.
- The Bible is an epic story of God's love and devotion for the people.
- Matthew 18 gives us a clear directive for handling dissident members with forgiveness and reconciliation as the goals.
- The generation we were born into influences our values and our world view.
- Recognize, discuss, and celebrate generational differences in values and views rather than allow them to generate conflict.

Chapter 3

Family Systems and Congregational Dynamics

If a family lives in harmony, all its affairs will prosper.

Chinese Proverb

At its monthly meeting, the Property Committee reviewed the request to consider air conditioning the sanctuary.

"How many years have we done without air conditioning? . . . 150 years!" said one member. "If we lasted that long without it, we don't need it now!"

"But what about the health of our congregation? So many of us have respiratory problems," pointed out another member. "Having AC might get more of us to church in the summer when attendance and contributions usually drop."

"Why spend all that money on air conditioning a church that will only be used one hour a week?" argued the first member. "It's just not worth it." Jane became frustrated with the continuing debate. This topic had come up before and always with the same results: arguments.

Tonight Jane was especially annoyed. Before the meeting, her husband had angrily approached her with questions over their family finances. He demanded to know why she had wasted their money on unbudgeted items, including clothes and novelties he said she didn't really need. Jane stormed out of the house. Now this—she was listening to more debates about money. This wasn't supposed to happen in church!

After a few minutes, Jane stood up and announced that she might resign from the committee. She picked up her coat. The door banged behind her as she left.

Jane grew up in a household that dodged conflict. Family members left the room or house when there were disagreements. Nothing was ever discussed or resolved. She continued that pattern in her marriage and in her participation at church.

The impact of personal or family issues

Congregations are incredibly complex. As individuals, we bring our own values and communication styles with us when we gather as a congregation. We also develop a group identity and group values. A lot of this is based on our communal history, including how conflicts have been handled within our congregation in the past. All this information becomes part of our collective personality as the people of God. Things get even stickier when we inadvertently blend our personal or family issues with the life of the congregation.

Jane had a hard time separating what had happened at home from what happened at the Property Committee meeting. For her, the arguments about money were one and the same. Her response to both situations followed her regular pattern: she avoided dealing with her husband and she avoided dealing with the committee. In both situations she just walked out. What do you think will happen when she returns home? What do you suppose she usually does after walking out on a conflict?

Systems theory looks at groups, including congregations, as complex emotional systems in which all the people involved are independent yet interconnected. The entire system is affected when the behavior or response of one person changes. The idea that congregations are emotional systems with dynamics similar to those operating in family systems has been studied very seriously since the publication of Edwin Friedman's *Generation to Generation: Family Process in Church and Synagogue* (New York: Guilford Press, 1985). This book provides a lens through which we can examine the life of a congregation. It enables us to look at our relationships and interactions within the community and how they contribute to the way the congregation functions.

There's no room for blaming individuals because if something unhealthy is going on in a family or a congregation, all the participants are letting it happen. We're all part of a system—at home and in the congregation. *Dysfunction*—ineffective or unhealthy interactions and communications between individuals or within a system—thrives only when we close our eyes or turn away.

Conflict and your family of origin

The way conflict was handled in your family of origin affects how you deal with it today. You probably learned your basic communication skills in the family. Even if you have worked to develop your skills beyond what you learned as a child, you probably still will have a strong pull to return to those first patterns when you become anxious and upset. That's why it's important to examine how conflict was handled in your household as you grew up.

The way conflict was handled in your family of origin affects how you deal with it today.

Exercise—Take some time to reflect on what you learned about conflict early in your life.

- What is the first family conflict you remember?
- What patterns for dealing with conflict developed in your household?
- Did family members pull the "dump and run" on each other by shouting their opinions and demands and then exiting so no one else could speak?
- Was there total shutdown, in which disagreements were ignored and never addressed?
- Did you play emotional "dodge ball," trying to avoid getting hit by casting blame on someone else?
- Who played what parts?
- Were disagreements resolved through discussion?

After you have looked at conflict and your family of origin, think about how you handle conflict today.

- How do you prefer to handle conflict at home and at church?
- Have you perpetuated the patterns you learned as a child, or have you made changes in your communication style?
- If you changed, what caused you to change?

Use the "Conflict and Your Family of Origin" tool on page 98 to consider how conflict was handled in your family of origin and discuss how that affects you and your leadership group.

Leave the dirty laundry at home

Calling ourselves the "family" of God doesn't give us permission to act out personal issues in a public forum.

It was easy for Jane to confuse what had happened at home and the disagreement at the Property Committee meeting. If someone enters a meeting angry because they have just argued with a spouse or child, the likelihood is high that their anger will show up in the dynamics of a meeting. The person might unload the anger on the group and dominate discussion by sharing their personal problems with the committee. They might get angry with someone else in the group and transfer the issues from home onto that person. Calling ourselves the "family" of God doesn't give us permission to act out personal issues in a public forum.

Assess some of the current issues in your personal life and how they might affect your leadership in the congregation with the "Personal Concerns" tool on pages 99-100. If you are a pastor, use the tool on pages 101-102.

Carrying our personal or family issues into the congregation can adversely affect the health and welfare of the congregation. Here are some ways that families might play out their disputes or concerns in public. Can you think of others?

- An argument between spouses or a divorce is played out in the congregation. Members are drawn into the conflict and take sides.
- Children act out in Sunday school, worship, and other church activities because of disruptive behavior and lack of necessary rules at home.

- The congregation begins to feel overly protective of certain members or the pastor because of their family or personal health issues. Factions may develop.
- A family that is a major contributor has adamant views about not starting a contemporary service. These wishes are upheld so that the family will not leave the congregation.

The ghosts of conflicts past

Major changes in the worship service, such as moving to a new hymnal or weekly communion, can be unsettling for a congregation. The care of the grounds and church building is always a potential troublemaker, especially if a large and unusual financial investment is required. "Space wars" can develop if no one keeps track of who is scheduled to use what room. And although the congregation belongs to Christ, generally people stake out their own space within a church building. (Have you ever accidentally sat in someone's regular pew? What was the reaction?)

Ghosts of conflicts past can affect your communal life in your congregation the same way that past conflicts from your family of origin can affect your current participation in family and church life. If a past traumatic controversy was not resolved, some type of avoidance may be operating in your congregation to this day. Once a cycle of denial gets started, it takes work to break it. If changing the look of the sanctuary caused severe problems 10 years ago, people may not want to tackle the issue again.

Once a cycle of denial gets started, it takes work to break it.

Identifying past conflicts in the congregation

Members of your congregation council can act as "conflict detectives" by discussing the dynamics of previous conflicts to detect patterns, especially in the area of conflict resolution. In a council meeting, list all the conflicts in your faith community that you can recall. Are there common themes in these conflicts? How were the

Larraine Frampton, Director of the ELCA (Evangelical Lutheran Church in America) Program for the Prevention of Clergy Sexual Abuse, has identified the following moments when conflict is most likely to occur in a congregation.

- A process for expressing concerns is not in place or is not periodically clarified.
- No committee is able to communicate with the pastor.
- The mission of the congregation is not clear or known.
- Bible study groups meet less than once a week.
- A congregational program review by synod or judicatory staff has not taken place for several years.
- There is a noticeable change in the leadership style of the new pastor or lay leaders.
- Membership has grown or decreased.
- Income has grown or decreased.
- There is no annual review of the congregation and pastor to evaluate how the mission statement is being met.
- There is a change in the church staff. Conflict can also arise if a new pastor arrives and staff members are kept in place but have no input on how they will work with the new pastor.
- The responsibilities of the congregation council are unclear.
- The size and configuration of the congregation council are not appropriate for the present size of the congregation.
- There are unresolved issues with previous pastors.
- Misconduct by leader(s) or member(s) is identified.
- The pastor is ill or on vacation.
- The congregation is celebrating a festival or holiday of the church.

conflicts resolved? Does the congregation have a pattern of resolving disputes or have some never been resolved?

If leaders of your congregation resist discussing past conflicts or if this is difficult for them, something in the past may be unresolved. If this is the case, ask your synod or judicatory staff if there are consultants or programs that might help your congregation work through an inquiry and healing process. In addition, trained facilitators are available to help your congregation look at the past and vision the future through Peter Steinke's Bridge Builders intervention process.

The pastor's influence in the system

As called leaders of a congregation, pastors can receive a lot of criticism for everything from the clothes they wear to the sermons they preach. Much of this criticism falls under the category of the absurd. Yet pastors need to realize that their interaction with the system has a profound effect on a congregation's health and interactions.

As Edwin Friedman points out in *Generation to Generation: Family Process in Church and Synagogue*, pastors can *overfunction* in their roles by assuming responsibility that others should take (New York: Guilford Press, 1985, pp. 210-211). Over-functioning usually involves crossing established boundaries. Pastors who over-function risk losing lay leadership and creating a dependence on the pastoral office. The temptation to over-function is high for clergy who feel a strong call to serve. On the other hand, if pastors dodge responsibility that belongs to them, this under-functioning can also create problems in the congregation.

Unresolved issues from one congregation may travel with a pastor to a new place.

It's rare today for a pastor to serve only one congregation during their entire career. Unresolved issues from one congregation may travel with a pastor to a new place, with history repeating itself in the new setting. The issue or content may be different, but the dynamics are the same.

Unresolved issues also can continue in a congregation after a pastor leaves. The desire to maintain a balance in the system is so strong that

If you are a pastor, look seriously at how you have handled responsibility in the congregations you have served. Since a lot of controversy arises in congregations over the role of the pastor, it pays to be aware of how responsible you feel for your congregation.

Do you get weighed down, blaming yourself when things go wrong? Do you dodge responsibility? What patterns do you see in your past behavior?

What major issues faced you in your last congregation? How did you resolve those issues? What did you do effectively? What would you do differently? What was your dominant feeling upon leaving your last call?

a pastor entering a new congregation may immediately be cast into the same role their predecessor played. The desire for the pattern to repeat itself is intense. It's important for pastors to pay attention to this dynamic because it indicates what may have transpired in the system in the past.

It is wise for a pastor and congregation to resolve as many issues as they can before the pastor leaves. A healthy and effective exit interview conducted between the pastor and congregation council can help the pastor and the congregation to carry less baggage into the future.

Freeing ourselves from the weight of the past

Jesus has freed us from the burden of our sins, and we have the promise of new life through him. That doesn't release us from seeking to be healthier and more effective human beings. Often when it comes to dealing with our past, we have some work to do.

What might happen next with Jane, the angry Property Committee member whose story began this chapter? What might she do to change the dynamics that have ruled her life? How easy do you think it would be for her to change? What might empower her to change her behavior?

Family systems theory tells us that if one individual within a family or system works to change themselves, that one change will have an effect on the entire system. If Mom has been the only one who does the cooking but then goes back to school for another degree, the family may end up changing the distribution of responsibilities. It works much the same in congregations. If a dominant member of a church committee decides to sit back and allow others to participate more fully, dynamics will shift.

Know thyself

What are areas that you need to work on as a leader? How do the issues you experience in your congregation connect with your family life issues? Is one bleeding into the other? How can you work to change yourself?

Boundaries are the necessary rules and limits of personal and group life, or the acceptable playing field in personal dynamics or a congregational system. When it comes to dealing with conflict, or just everyday life, it is important to know who you are and where your personal boundaries begin and end. Systems theory refers to this as *self-differentiation*, the ability to self-define by developing self-knowledge, setting clear personal boundaries, and making "I" statements while communicating with others. Self-differentiation was summed up by the ancient Greeks in two words: *Know thyself.*

Recognize your personal boundaries and those of others.

In congregational leadership, either lay or clergy, many people will try to tell you who you are and what your job is. Knowing your boundaries is critical. You need to know where your personal and vocational responsibility begins and ends. You should also recognize your personal boundaries and those of others. Any time someone else defines you, they have crossed your boundaries—sometimes the crossing is small and sometimes it's huge.

Part of self-differentiation is the ability to take a stand and acknowledge our boundaries, beliefs, and limitations. As Peter Steinke points out in *How Your Church Family Works: Understanding Congregations as Emotional Systems* (Alban Institute, 1993, p. 81), Martin Luther's famous quote at the Diet of Worms is an example of self-differentiation: "Here I stand, I can do no other, so help me God."

Notice that Luther's statement is about "I." When we use "I" statements, we define ourselves. When we use "you" statements, we define others. Stick to "I" statements and you'll be on the right track to healthier communications. Self-differentiated leaders do not cut themselves off, but instead stay connected with others. (See chapter 5 for more information on healthy communications.) If people are talking with each other, they are connected and have a basis on which to resolve problems large and small.

Stick to "I" statements and you'll be on the right track to healthier communications.

Journaling, self-assessments, and counseling can all help you keep in touch with who you are as a leader of the congregation. Know your core beliefs and convictions as a leader and as a person. Ask yourself if there is a conflict between the two. A congregation is an incredibly complex system in which the interactions between people in the system eventually give the congregation its own personality. As leaders, our goal is to keep that interaction as healthy as possible to empower our church community to better witness to the love of God.

Summary

- Our communication skills and how we view conflict are initially learned in our family of origin.
- Self-awareness is needed since our tendency under high stress is to revert back to those patterns we learned in our family of origin.
- Individual family dysfunctions can enter into the life of a congregation if allowed by the congregation.
- Ghosts of past congregational conflicts can haunt a congregation if left unresolved.
- As the called leaders, pastors have significant influence on the system and should seek to maintain healthy relationships at home and at church.
- Pastors should seek to resolve issues with congregations upon their departure so that the issues do not continue in the congregation or carry into their new ministries.

Chapter 4

Community Conflict

Man must evolve for all human conflict a method
which rejects revenge, aggression and retaliation.
The foundation of such a method is love.

Martin Luther King Jr., 1964 Nobel Peace Prize acceptance speech

An angry Social Ministry chairperson approaches you after a worship service because "somebody" cleaned the bulletin boards and removed his notice for an important upcoming event. He accuses the sexton of overstepping his bounds and doing this because the two of them haven't gotten along in years. Then he stomps off.

Fighting in the dark: community conflict

You've just discovered that an unofficial "phone chain" has been seeking to block the congregation council's recommendation to hire a youth ministry worker. The congregational meeting is in two weeks, and you're not sure what to do. The battle lines are drawn. One side is focused on the young people of the congregation. The other side is angry about spending money to hire another person and feels the pastor should be doing more in the area of youth ministry.

Recognizing that a conflict is headed in the wrong direction can help us deal with a situation before it gets too far out of control. Watch for triangulation, boundary violations, unmanaged polarities, an increased level of the conflict, and the decline of the spiritual community.

Triangulation: the blame game

Triangulation occurs when two people aren't relating in a healthy manner and aren't comfortable with each other, so one of them—

usually the most anxious—draws in a third party. The two people fighting even blame the third party for what is happening. Spouses who aren't getting along might blame a child's acting up for their problems. Triangulation also occurs when someone draws in a third party in order to gain personal security and release anxiety by unloading concerns on an ally. If the administrative assistant is upset with the workload that the pastor has given her, she might seek out an ally by complaining to the Christian Education Director or another member of the church staff.

Secrets and hidden agendas are definitely signs of unhealthy conflict or fighting in the dark.

Triangulation is indirect and unfair communication. At least one of the parties who should be speaking to the other is dodging effective communication. When people aren't talking directly to each other, there is a problem. In the story of the phone chain, whoever started calling people to complain about the hiring of a new youth minister was uncomfortable with the council's action and wanted to gain support before the congregational meeting. Secrets and hidden agendas are definitely signs of unhealthy conflict or fighting in the dark.

Boundaries: Who's on first?

When nobody knows who is responsible for anything, people are living together without boundaries. There is mass confusion, and ministry is not effective. People start stepping on each other's toes, which can cause conflict to escalate.

In the life of a congregation, boundaries may be violated for several reasons. Individuals who have a deep-seated need for control or fear of being out of control may only feel comfortable when they take over. Others may lose a sense of the line between their personal life and the life of the congregation due to a poor sense of boundaries. This is called *fusion*, the loss of emotional or physical boundaries between individuals or between individuals and systems. Fusion can happen with clergy or lay leaders who feel so responsible for a congregation that they are always in the church building or always working. When a person fuses with a congregation, personal issues can bleed into the congregational system or vice versa.

Frequent boundary violations usually are a sign that there is a problem within the congregation's leadership structure. Boundary violations don't just happen—people let them happen. Everyone should know the appropriate playing field and stay within their defined bounds. Things will run more smoothly and there will be less need for time-outs.

Polarities: never the twain shall meet

Sometimes there are conflicts or situations that have no real possibility for a definitive resolution. These are called polarities. According to Barry Johnson, author of *Polarity Management: Identifying and Managing Unsolvable Problems* (Amherst, Mass.: HRD Press, 1996, p. xviii), polarities have two main characteristics. They are interdependent and they are conflicts that do not end. They can't be resolved because both are necessary in relationship with each other. It's like yin and yang, up and down, left and right. Which one is better when they are both necessary?

Polarities can turn into unhealthy conflicts when people falling on either side of the pole do not acknowledge the legitimacy of the other side. Then the conflict becomes a battle of wills and it is likely that no one will budge.

Johnson recommends graphing out the polarity with either pole on a horizontal line. Add a vertical plus and minus axis. Johnson says that to manage a polarity well, one must attempt to focus on the positive aspects of both sides of the polarity and work within those quadrants (*Polarity Management: Identifying and Managing Unsolvable Problems*, p. 81). If individuals on either side of the polarity can recognize the positive in the other side, that's a step in the right direction.

For example, in a Lutheran understanding of who we are as people of God, law and gospel are both necessary. A polarity chart for law and gospel might look like the one on the next page.

In this example, if you are stuck in one of the negative quadrants, you would focus on the quadrant diagonally across from it to manage the polarity. If you are feeling unworthy and burdened by sin, move to

Boundary violations don't just happen.

+	+
Helps us recognize our sinfulness	Releases us from bondage to sin
Makes us aware of our need for God	Promises forgiveness and new life in Christ
Law	**Gospel**
−	−
May cause us to feel burdened by our sins	May not fully recognize our sinfulness
May result in feelings of worthlessness	May result in belief that we can do whatever we want because God loves us

recognize the freedom, forgiveness, and new life that we receive through Christ. If you believe you can do whatever you want, focus on the need for us to recognize our sinfulness and need for God.

What issues do you see as true polarities in your congregation? Some might be participation in local congregation/participation in the synod or church-at-large, responsibility for the welfare of the community/care for needy individuals, or repentance/forgiveness. If your congregation or group is dealing with a polarity, create a polarity chart. Encourage people to acknowledge the positive aspects of each pole.

The level and intensity of conflict: molehills or mountains

Following worship, a member of your congregation loudly complains that the acolyte was wearing sneakers and the first-time visitors might never return because of it. How would you respond to this?

Most complaints that involve one or two people are just that. There is no need to stress out over isolated incidents and complaints like these. Talk to the person who has complained, find out what's really bothering him or her, but don't sweat it.

There is a proposal to build an addition to the church building for a fellowship hall and additional rooms for the expanding Sunday school. Factions develop in the congregation and the last meeting of the congregation council involved several heated arguments. This is a mountain that needs careful attention.

Keep in mind that groups within the congregation can be indicative of the mood of the congregation at large. If the members of the congregation council are fighting with each other, this might reflect the current emotional state of the congregation.

The more people involved in the conflict, the bigger the problem. When more people are involved, the level of conflict has increased and a web of triangulation has occurred. The likelihood is greater that everyone is tied up and will need to work hard to get free.

It's also true that the more intense the conflict, the bigger the problem. When disagreements over goals, values, and needs lead to put-downs of others, taking sides, or trying to eliminate individuals from the situation, the intensity of the conflict has increased.

When the level or intensity of conflict is increasing, anxiety may be present throughout the congregational system. Outside consultation or support may be needed. Take these situations seriously.

When conflict goes without attention, resolution, or reconciliation, the body of Christ suffers.

Decline in the spiritual community: holding grudges

Ongoing conflict in the life of a congregation often has to do with holding grudges. It shows a lack of forgiveness. In one congregation, for example, there were some problems with the Christmas program several years ago and one or two people bring this up every fall when plans for the next program are discussed.

When conflict goes without attention, resolution, or reconciliation, the body of Christ suffers. You can see signs immediately. Worship attendance drops off. There is a general feeling of malaise. People withhold their pledges and donations. Leaders may find it hard to motivate themselves, let alone others. Clergy may have trouble sleeping or getting out of bed in the morning. Nothing feels like it's going well—and it's not. There is an infection in the body that needs attention.

Every leader's nightmare is dealing with conflict that has ripped through a community causing fighting and bitter factions. It's better to seek to continually develop healthy elements for dealing with conflict.

Healthy conflict

Conflict happens. This is a reality of life. But how do we stop conflict from becoming a destructive force? How do we seek to live the imperative to love one another, even if we are having trouble understanding each other and getting along? The challenge is to use conflict as a growing edge rather than as something that divides us.

The first priority is to try to keep all conflict above board and in the light. Once conflict goes underground, the path to destruction has already begun.

High anxiety can lead to an escalation in conflict. When you're upset, you don't think as logically and clearly as usual. When two or more highly anxious people get together, things are almost certain to get out of control. The room is flooded with electricity, not logic. The sooner you can get all parties talking to each other the better, because that allows less time for anxiety to escalate.

We're used to hearing that Christians shouldn't disagree at all, but the fact is that we're human.

As people, we have differences in our experiences and values. Sometimes we don't get along or understand each other.

When we learn to deal with conflict in healthy ways, we can disagree without deliberately trying to hurt each other.

This takes respect, direct communication, boundaries, humor, and forgiveness.

R-E-S-P-E-C-T

The number-one element of healthy conflict in a congregation or anywhere else is learning to respect each other. That's probably one of our hardest lessons as humans. When we respect other people, we accept where they are and what they think at any moment in time. Often those thoughts and feelings do not agree with our own, so we need to step outside of our own framework. Respect involves listening to others with the intention of seeking to understand them.

This doesn't give permission for one person to order everyone around. That's control, and control is never based on respect. Control is focused on "me," on the needs or wants of one person. But respect is a reciprocal sharing of communication, thoughts, and concerns.

Sometimes when you understand the opinion of another person more clearly, you still disagree. Agreeing to disagree with someone on the hymns or style of worship you prefer is okay. You are both entitled to your opinions. The trick is to work so that those opinions do not prevent you from further healthy communication.

One way to practice respect is to ask questions—lots of questions—to seek to learn more about the opinions another person holds.

Another step in learning to respect is to pray for the other person as a brother or sister in Christ. In prayer, acknowledge your commonality and your mutual need for God's love and grace. That's one less wall that will divide you.

Respect is a reciprocal sharing of communication, thoughts, and concerns.

Direct communication

When we seek to approach someone from a position of respect, we do so not by talking about that person, but by speaking directly with him or her about matters that concern or confuse us. If you are upset or don't understand a comment a council member makes at a meeting, what are your options? You could go home and call others to complain or you could call the person directly to ask about their words. Calling the person directly is a good move. Better yet, you could respectfully ask questions of clarification at the meeting.

**The books
*Our Structure:
Carrying Out the
Vision* and
*Our Staff:
Building Our
Human Resources*
contain more
information on
committee
expectations and
job descriptions.**

The indirect approach probably trips us up the most. When we are upset, we often unload our emotions on someone—a spouse, friend, or another church member—and avoid the person with whom we really need to speak.

Don't approach another person in anger, however. You're less likely to follow the first guideline of respect when you are angry. In addition, anger can breed more anger and it keeps us from the type of questioning and listening we should be doing in order to better understand the other person. Be calm and direct to bring about healthy communication.

In times of serious conflict or crisis in a congregation, emotions can run high. Direct communication may fail to bring about a resolution. In situations like these, ask your synod or judicatory staff for assistance.

Boundaries

When a ball is thrown out of bounds in basketball, the game comes to a halt until it is tossed back onto the court where it belongs. That can happen in congregations, too. When someone oversteps the boundaries of their responsibilities, ministry can come to a halt until things get sorted out and everyone gets back in position.

The Evangelism Committee decides on a date to canvass the neighborhood near the church. After the arrangements are made, one member of the committee decides to change the date because it wasn't good for them. You will certainly have confusion and probably a bit of conflict over this. When one person alters the plans of a committee, the committee's structure and authority are undermined.

**Boundaries
give us a
framework
in which to
operate.**

Boundaries give us a framework in which to operate. They provide an acceptable playing field. Agree upon who is responsible for what task. As a leader of the congregation, know the limits of your own responsibility. Let the pastor function as pastor. Let committee chairs do their jobs. If someone comes to you with a complaint about the Stewardship Committee, be sure it's your responsibility to handle it

Job descriptions

When people do not know the expectations and limits of their responsibilities in the congregation, troubles will arise.

- A well-intentioned administrative assistant tells a lonely congregation member who is homebound that the pastor will visit the next day, but the pastor's schedule is already filled for that day.

- A Worship and Music Committee member happens to be in a Christian bookstore and decides to pick up bulletins for the upcoming Ash Wednesday service, but the church administrative assistant ordered the same bulletins months ago.

One way to cut down on conflicts caused by overstepping bounds is to make sure that employee and committee job descriptions are in place. Put the responsibilities in writing. Make sure all of the appropriate parties agree on it.

Review job descriptions annually and make adjustments if necessary. Then stick to them and there will be fewer problems.

See chapter 6 for more details on how to develop clearly stated expectations for all ministry positions.

before you get involved. Ask yourself: Is this really my job? Why do I feel responsible?

Humor

A pastor pours wine from a large flask into the chalice or cup. While tipping the flask, the lid falls off and lands in the chalice. The pastor chuckles as he pulls the lid out.

A boy sees his mother in the choir and runs down the side aisle to give her a hug and a kiss.

A lot of things that happen in our life as a community in Christ can be cute and sometimes just plain funny. However, things that are out of the ordinary can greatly upset people who prefer a more structured routine. Sometimes these things turn into conflict issues, like the missing poster for the social ministry event or the little boy running in church.

Conflict can escalate when people take themselves too seriously. But sometimes we need to lighten up a bit. Humor can diffuse a tense moment or situation.

In *Telling the Truth: The Gospel as Tragedy, Comedy, and Fairy Tale*, Frederick Buechner wrote: "Is it possible, I wonder, to say that it is only when you hear the Gospel as a wild and marvelous joke that you really hear it at all?" Look for the humor in your day and celebrate it. Go ahead and laugh and imagine God smiling that you got the joke.

Forgiveness

Healthy conflict includes the expectation of forgiveness and reconciliation, a coming together where misunderstanding or harsh words once divided us. Reconciliation starts with each individual practicing the act of forgiveness.

Even the smallest conflict left unattended can fester.

Forgiveness doesn't dwell on the past. It acknowledges the problems and then moves beyond them. You can't change what happened in the past, but you can set boundaries for how you will interact in the present and move ahead. As people of God, we sometimes forget that we are forgiven and are called to share that forgiveness with others. It's not ours to keep for ourselves. It's meant to be shared.

When in the middle of a disagreement with someone, try to focus on the God who unifies you and not on whatever divides you. Look for areas of agreement. Often we are so focused on the conflict that we forget we may have much in common.

Even if the other party doesn't want to be reconciled, and sometimes that will happen, you can forgive them. Release the burden that binds your heart and you will be freed to love even those who do not love you.

Even the smallest conflict left unattended can fester. In the example at the beginning of this chapter, the fact that the chairperson referred to past problems is a sign of unresolved issues. Chances are high that the poster was removed in error, but lack of clarity over who is to clean bulletin boards also may be a problem.

How might you introduce the five elements of healthy conflict into this or any conflict to diffuse the anger?

Use the "Congregational Conflict Monitor" tool on pages 103-105 to discuss the current status of your congregation and how you might move more fully into the light.

The biblical imperative

When dealing with community conflict, we need to proceed from the biblical imperative to love one another and remember the words of Paul: "Love is patient; love is kind; love is not envious or boastful

---

What forgiveness is . . . and isn't

Forgiveness is . . .

- Confession in which the offending party recognizes the sin and with a contrite heart admits it to the injured party.
- Repentance in which the offender changes behavior as a result of the confession.
- Reconciliation with both parties agreeing upon guidelines for their future interaction to prevent a repeat of past conflicts.
- Restoration of a relationship—perhaps even better than before because you've weathered a storm together.
- Acknowledgment of what happened, how it changed you, and the decision to move on.
- Always rooted in God's love for each of us.

Forgiveness isn't . . .

- Permission to continue inappropriate or hurtful behavior.
- Ignoring a destructive situation because you're afraid to make it worse.
- Reminding the offender of your grace in "forgiving" them.
- Dredging up the past.

or arrogant or rude. It does not insist on its own way; it is not irritable or resentful; it does not rejoice in wrongdoing, but rejoices in truth. It bears all things, believes all things, hopes all things, endures all things" (1 Corinthians 13:4-7).

Love communicates above board and in the light of Christ's love. Love is not anxious, but hopeful. Always.

Summary

Love communicates above board and in the light of Christ's love.

- Signs of unhealthy conflict are: triangulation, frequent boundary violations, unmanaged polarities, increases in the level or intensity of conflict, and the decline of the spiritual community.
- Polarities are conflicts that cannot be resolved, only managed.
- Healthy conflict is above board and stays in the light.
- The five elements of healthy conflict are: *respect*, *direct communication*, *boundaries*, *humor*, and *forgiveness*.
- Humor is a gift from God to keep us from taking ourselves too seriously.
- Deal with congregational conflict on the basis of love.

Chapter 5

Learning Life Skills

Handle them carefully,
for words have more power than atom bombs.

Pearl Strachan Hurd, from *The Christian Science Monitor*

Remember that childhood adage: "Sticks and stones can break my bones but words can never hurt me"? If only that were true. But words and our interpretations of them *do* hurt us at times. When that happens, our emotions can get in the way and conflict can escalate. That's why one of the most critical life skills is communication. This includes recognizing that what we mean to say may not be what another person actually hears.

Our listening skills and life experiences affect what we actually hear. Personal experiences can result in an internal filter for communication. For example, the image of God as a loving parent may be incomprehensible to a person who was physically or emotionally abused by a parent. Our discussion of the church as the "family" of God could actually sound judgmental to a person who is single.

A congregation council meeting brings together several people, all with different listening skills and a variety internal filters. It takes work for everyone to be on the same wavelength when discussing anything, whether it be a possible change to weekly communion or the purchase of property.

Three steps for effective communication

Here are three steps to more effective communicating: *reflect*, *analyze*, and *respond*.

Reflect

Most of us have at least one mirror in our homes that we use to check our appearance before starting the day. We make sure everything is in place before we proceed.

Communicating involves listening to others and then reflecting back to them what we have heard. Unless we've shared many life experiences and have developed a common vocabulary, chances are high that that our understandings of life and the world around us will be different. Even couples who have lived together for years will still have different interpretations of conversations and events. They, too, need to check their interpretations with one another in the course of daily living.

It pays to mirror back what we hear and check it out.

Reflecting means we acknowledge the life experience and internal filters of another person. We respect them and, like looking in the mirror, check out their perspective.

Reflective listening means being in touch with where you are and what you are hearing. Then you claim it and ask questions.

When the level of trust is high and the intensity of emotions is low, you could inquire by asking, "Did you mean such and such?" or "What did you mean when you said . . .?" A better method is to let the other person know what you heard. This is an acknowledgment of where you're at and how you're interpreting things. Try asking, "What I heard you saying is . . . ? Is that what you meant?" Ask questions that clarify meanings, not questions that accuse.

Reflective listening is one of those things that we usually skip over in the heat of an argument. We jump to conclusions when, in fact, we and the other person may be closer to agreement than we realize. It pays to mirror back what we hear and check it out. We could cut short a misunderstanding and come to a new, common understanding. Or, at the very least, we might hear more clearly what another person is seeking to share with us. That's certainly worth the effort.

Analyze

"I've been hearing that you don't make hospital visits, Pastor," said the council vice president. "Two people have been in the hospital this past month and both of them told me that you didn't see them. What are you going to do about fulfilling your responsibilities to this congregation to do pastoral visitations?"

This is a common complaint, but what's the real issue here? The lack of pastoral visitations? Possibly. More information needs to be obtained, however, before that determination can be made. You can never assume that what is being stated is really the issue that needs to be addressed.

Was the pastor ever notified of the hospitalization? Was a request for a visit ever made? According to the guidelines to healthy conflict (in chapter 4), direct communication is best. That's true for all communications on all occasions.

In *Generation to Generation*, Edwin Friedman identifies a variety of issues in congregations that can get focused on the clergy. Everything from the pastor's attitude to taste in clothes can and at some point probably will be discussed. But there may be something else happening. The trick is to listen carefully and analyze the issues.

Some issues are actually smoke screens intended to distract leaders.

Some issues are actually smoke screens intended to distract leaders when a congregation is on the threshold of potential change or growth. Friedman identifies these as *content* issues. Content issues cause a congregation to become overly focused on issues such as preaching style, administrative capabilities, or the family of the pastor. This can tie you and your congregation up in knots. That means nobody's going anywhere.

Asking the following questions can help you determine if you are dealing with a content issue:
- How did this issue come about?
- Is the issue focused on the pastor or another significant leader in the congregation? If it is, it may be a content issue.

- What else is happening in the life of the congregation that might be contributing to the pursuit of the stated issue?
- Is there something else going on in the life of the person who is complaining that may be spilling over into the life of the congregation?
- What potential program or change in the church might be derailed by focusing on this issue?
- Is more reflective listening needed?

These are all questions that congregational leaders need to analyze before simply concluding that the pastor needs to make more visits. In the meantime, make sure the process for notifying the pastor of desired visitations is clearly and regularly stated in newsletters and bulletins. A proactive stance is always a strong one.

Respond

In the midst of conflict, it is important to slow things down.

Although we're often tempted to make this our first step in communicating, response is really the third step. Reflection and analysis need to come first. In the midst of conflict, it is important to slow things down. Take time to listen, analyze, and then respond. This will cut down on reactive damage control, the "let's get it over with as soon as possible" responses that are seldom effective and may in fact be quite destructive.

What's a reactive response? Well, let's look at the example of the complaint about pastoral visitations. Several people could make reactive responses to this complaint. The pastor might take it personally and say, "I'm offended that you would question my pastoral leadership and visitations!" Another council member might say, "Pastor, you need to let us know exactly who you are visiting and when. Then we can nip this thing in the bud." The pastor would be letting emotion rule her response while the second council member would be jumping to a solution before understanding the dynamics of what is occurring at the meeting and in the congregation.

Don't let content issues derail you, especially amid important changes. To handle an issue like the complaint about visitations, make sure the congregation knows the appropriate process to use (for example, how to contact the pastor when there is a hospitalization). Publish the policy or procedure in the congregation's newsletters and weekly bulletins. Hold members accountable if they have not followed procedure, yet still complain.

A proactive response is still more effective. Communication problems that occur in groups within a congregation, such as committees, might be indicative of a larger malaise. Pay attention to what is going on in these groups and in the congregation.

It's a good idea for council members to take regular "readings" of the congregation and its committees or working groups. Where is the pressure or temperature rising within the congregation? What might be causing this? These questions could be asked as a standard part of each council meeting to clue you in to potential problems before they surface and address situations before they get out of hand.

Creating guidelines for communication

Another proactive step is to work on guidelines for communication within your congregation. Discussing your plans for better communications gives birth to the very thing that it seeks to create. In the process itself we obtain our goal—healthier communications. Everybody wins when that happens.

What "rules" of communication do you need to establish within your congregation?

What "rules" of communication already exist within your congregation? Are there particular areas that need fine-tuning? What "rules" of communication do you need to establish within your congregation? Although it may seem strange to consider creating guidelines for relating to one another, this is an opportunity to discuss the creation of a vocabulary and internal filter for your community. It is also an opportunity to clarify what is appropriate and when behavior is out of bounds.

The awareness that communication takes work is always a good thing. When we learn to respect the way in which we use words in our communications, we end up learning to respect one another.

Summary

Use the tool on pages 106-108 to identify examples of "I" statements and "you" statements.

- What people hear depends on their listening skills and internal filters.
- Effective communication takes work.
- There are three steps to more effective communicating: *reflect*, *analyze*, and *respond*.
- Reflective listening seeks clarification on what we have heard.
- Analysis of the stated issues prevents content issues from binding the congregation.
- Responses should be thoughtful and not reactive.
- Communally agreed upon guidelines for communication give your church a common vocabulary and internal filter.

12 guidelines for more effective communications

When faced with ineffective congregational communications, one congregation council discussed and voted on the following guidelines, which were then posted on bulletin boards and in the newsletter.

1. Test all your assumptions verbally.
2. Ask questions instead of making judgments.
3. Recognize that each event can be seen from different points of view.
4. Own your feelings and perceptions. Use "I" statements rather than "you" statements.
5. Be open and honest about your feelings.
6. Do not use unfair communication techniques, such as manipulation and baiting.
7. Accept all feelings and seek to understand them.
8. Do not engage in gossip. Speak directly to the people concerned.
9. Do not allow discussions to turn into destructive arguments. If you start heading down the wrong path, stop and redirect the discussion.
10. Be tactful, considerate, and courteous.
11. Hold each other accountable for group decisions.
12. Trust in the presence of the Holy Spirit and seek to extend that trust to others.

Adapted from "Rules of Communication," by Herb Stroup and Norma Wood, from "Marriage and Family Counseling" course at the Lutheran Theological Seminary at Gettysburg, 1983.

Chapter 6

Surviving the Storms

'Tis the set of a soul
that decides its goal,
And not the calm or the strife.

Ella Wheeler Wilcox, "The Winds of Fate"

As a leader, you stand at the helm of the good ship *Our Congregation*. Violent waves crash over the rails onto the deck. The ship convulses uncontrollably. You fear the whole vessel will capsize. All hands hold on for dear life. When will the tempest end? Will you even survive? That's the feeling of unhealthy conflict raging out of control. At its worst, it threatens to tear apart the hull of your congregational life. At the very least, it shakes your personal faith life. This is especially true if you are a leader.

Leaders usually take the brunt of conflict. It comes with the territory. When unhealthy conflict rages, leaders must stay focused on their individual tasks and their corporate direction. It's not unusual for those caught up in the conflict to pit leaders against each other in the triangulation game. In addition, blame may be tossed about in an attempt to see who will react to it, or better yet, blindly accept it.

Three critical areas of leadership in a congregation are the pastor(s), congregation council, and the committees or ministry teams. If you are in one of these leadership roles you eventually will deal with, and may become the target of, some form of conflict. Because of this, it's important for you to know your role and its focus. The crew will function best when leaders all know their places and fulfill them, even in the fiercest hail, wind, or rain.

The pastor

Worship attendance has dropped over the past several months and you're not sure why. There are rumors that some people don't like the pastor's sermons and new style of worship leadership. If you're the pastor, this conflict has three potential ingredients to knock you off track and cause you to lose focus:

1. Nobody likes to be the target. It's an uncomfortable and often even painful position in which to be. Our tendency is to look for the fastest path out of the line of fire when it is directed at us. We may prematurely abandon our sense of direction and priorities, even if they were constructive, just to end our pain.

2. It's easy to fall into the guilt trap. We often forget that conflict is a normal part of life, including congregational life. In addition, pastors often feel that the existence of any conflict in the congregation shows a deficit in their leadership. This leads to questions like these: "What have we done wrong?" and "Why is this happening now?" Pastors may end up accepting the blame for a content issue, even if it is really irrelevant.

3. Pastors and staff members pursue their vocations because they feel called by God to serve. Conflict, especially the presence of severe and extended conflict, can shake an individual's spirituality and faith. It can cause leaders to question their calls.

Jesus has final authority over the storm that terrifies the disciples.

Focus on Jesus

We can get so caught up in disputes that we forget that the boat isn't really ours to own and to control. We are but caretakers. When the boat is rocking and the storms seem relentless, read the account of Jesus stilling the storm in Mark 4:35-41. There are two important lessons for pastoral leaders here.

First, Jesus has final authority over the storm that terrifies the disciples. Although things look very much out of control, they are not. Remember that it is fear that causes us to panic. In the midst of the storm, we need to work on controlling our own fears as leaders so that we are more effective.

Second, hear the words "Peace! Be Still!" Leaders caught in the midst of conflict often have the tendency to become both reactive and hyperactive in word and in deed. This is especially true if you become the target. When you begin to mimic the storm with your actions and words, it can engulf you. Jesus' words are meant to calm the storm in you, too: "Peace! Be still."

When the winds blow and the waves crash, be still and listen for the voice of the One who has ultimate authority over the storm. Remember that as the pastor you are called to preach, teach, and administer the sacraments. That role is never more important than in the midst of conflict. For it is in the conflict that we not only lose sight of the shore, but of our purpose and meaning.

Speak the promise and power of God's love and forgiveness, and believe it.

As a pastor, you can share Jesus' real presence and power with the worshiping community through Word and Sacrament. Members of the congregation need to know that God loves them even when they're not getting along. They need to know that love will empower the congregation to find solutions to problems. Speak the promise and power of God's love and forgiveness, and believe it. It's meant for you, too.

Remember that conflict happens

When we recognize and accept that conflict is a natural event in the life of the congregation, we can learn how to better navigate it. Remember that each birth has its own birth pains. You can expect that when things are going well, something will happen. When a balance is shifted by a change in the operations of a congregation, there will be an attempt to stabilize and move back to the familiar. This response is called *homeostasis*. It is the strong desire and pull of a system not to change but instead to maintain what is comfortable and familiar.

Each change and each motion forward has the potential to cause conflict. The congregation council spends time on developing a new

Tough questions

The pastor can often be the focus of conflict in a congregation. If you are a pastor, you will need to ask yourself some tough questions when conflict arises. Have you in any way facilitated the conflict?

For example, if the complaint is about the change in preaching style, you should ask yourself if you have spent less time in sermon-preparation lately.

It's also important to be aware of any conflict preferences that you carry from your family of origin. Review chapter 3 to reflect upon your feelings about conflict in general.

The more aware you are of where you are at, the better you'll be at avoiding baits and traps in disputes.

method of internal church and committee communications so everyone knows what's happening each month in the congregation—but few committees actually use it. A stricter newsletter deadline is set to improve work flow, but important notices still show up in the secretary's box two days late.

Don't be surprised that there is backsliding. If anything, try to outsmart it. What contingencies can the leader put in place? How can new plans be strengthened as they are implemented?

Depersonalize the conflict

Clergy are the prophets of the gathered community. Just like prophets, at times clergy will be the focus of attack. When complaints about the sermons, leadership style, and other choices surface, ask what is really going on. Don't get caught on the surface, but dig deeper.

Family systems theory tells us that anxiety in a group often focuses itself on either the most responsible or the most vulnerable individuals. If anxiety and blame within a congregation focuses on the leadership, either pastoral or lay, there is a reason worth discovering.

Ask questions to depersonalize the conflict:

- How relevant is the issue to the goals of the mission of the congregation?
- Is the attack a distinctly personal attack? If so, what motivation might there be to attack the pastor or lay leaders?
- How might focusing on the issue throw the current direction of ministry off course?
- Why is the issue important now?

Stay out of the line of fire

After worship, a disagreement breaks out between two council members. As the pastor, you witness this and feel a need to do something. Do you have feelings of guilt or discomfort that an argument just happened in your congregation between two leaders? Do you have an overwhelming feeling of responsibility for whatever goes on in the church building? Do you think others expect you to get involved just because you are the pastor?

Isn't it ironic that while we dislike being the target of conflict, as leaders we often feel obligated to jump into the fray when it starts around us? By overfunctioning, pastors can actually prolong a conflict. You may be on the phone with the council president, planning a meeting to discuss the issues you heard while the two members have already reached an agreement! As far as they are concerned, things may be resolved.

We can't apologize for others or try to smooth things over. As leaders, we need to allow people to be responsible for their own actions and words. When we don't do this, we may become the very thing that prevents their growth and extends a conflict.

Allow people to be responsible for their own actions and words.

A unique role: the afterpastor

Revelations of sexual misconduct on the part of clergy has given the church a new term for a pastor who follows in the wake—the *afterpastor.* In an essay titled "Afterpastors in Troubled Congregations" (*Restoring the Soul of a Church: Healing Congregations Wounded by*

Clergy Sexual Misconduct. Collegeville, Minnesota: Liturgical Press, 1995, p. 155), Darlene K. Haskin writes that the term *afterpastor* originated with a support group for pastors who served parishes after cases of clergy sexual misconduct.

A congregation that has been the secondary victim of a case of betrayal of the pastoral office is likely to face elevated levels of conflict. The congregation often suffers from feelings of shame and extensive distrust of the pastoral office. This distrust may extend to all authority in the congregation, including the lay leadership. As one afterpastor put it, "They do not trust themselves anymore because they were duped for such a long time."

The congregation may try to take power away from the afterpastor in a variety of ways. There is a tendency to hold meetings (especially finance meetings) and not notify the new pastor. It is much harder for this pastor to enter the system and find acceptance because the system closes down to protect itself from the previous betrayal. Afterpastors will often find themselves the focus of anger, projection, and scapegoating. This may happen if the truth of what transpired has not ever been spoken in the congregation.

Afterpastors will often find themselves the focus of anger, projection, and scapegoating.

In the book *Restoring the Soul of a Church*, Nancy Myer Hopkins recommends a reality check for afterpastors under attack. If the intensity of the attack upon you is much greater than that of other congregations you've served, then the likelihood is greater that projection or scapegoating is occurring.

The need for self-care on the part of afterpastors is higher than in other more normally functioning congregations:

- The afterpastor needs a very high degree of self-differentiation.
- All of the afterpastor's family issues need to be addressed.
- The afterpastor should see a therapist or spiritual counselor on a regular basis for a place to debrief, as there is always something happening in the congregation.
- The afterpastor needs to work out all personal issues. The system is often so strong that it will find and use the worst nightmares of afterpastors.

- Afterpastors must have a very strong support system outside of the church.

The same congregational dynamics at work in a congregation that has had a case of clergy sexual misconduct could also be present in a congregation that has had any severe breach of pastoral ethics, such as embezzlement or substance abuse.

The congregation council

Let's look at the conflict over the drop in worship attendance and the focus on the pastor's preaching and leadership style from the perspective of the congregation council. This conflict has some ingredients that could cause the council to lose focus, too.

The triangulation of the pastor as the person being blamed could cause the council to focus on a content issue and therefore on the pastor. Quick fixes might be suggested, such as a change in worship or preaching style. Is that really the issue or is something else going on? This is worth considering.

Role confusion may lead the council to dictate worship changes. If the congregation has called the pastor to oversee worship, possibly in conjunction with a Worship and Music Committee, to dictate to the pastor in this area would undermine her authority.

Lack of unity is always a danger in conflicted situations. Disgruntled council members may extend a conflict by complaining outside the meeting room about group decisions. This is never healthy.

Open your meetings with a time of sharing joys and concerns.

Build trust and community

If members of the central leadership body of a congregation don't trust each other and get along, how can you expect the rest of the congregation to begin to do so? It's critical, especially during conflict, to work on developing trust and a spirit of cooperation among your congregational leaders.

Build relationships. Take time to get to know each other. Open your meetings with a time of sharing joys and concerns. Assign prayer partners or days on which each person prays for specific council members. Pray for each other regularly. You're in this together.

Create a council covenant and put it in writing. In the very creation of the covenant, you achieve an important goal—discussion and agreement on who you are as leaders and what is and is not acceptable behavior and styles of communication. See the sample covenant for ideas. Discuss it as a group. Vote on your covenant and sign it. Post it where all can see it. Consider including it in the congregational newsletter. Review it annually as each new council is elected. Make changes as necessary. Read it in the congregation when council members are installed. It will send a strong message of unity.

Stick together

A congregation council should feel free to dialogue and disagree around the meeting table. Each member's opinion is important. Listen,

---

Sample: "Covenant of commitment, trust, and communication"

We, as the members of the congregation council of _____, out of concern for the health of Christ's Body do covenant the following with one another:

For the duration of my elected term, I will fulfill my commitment as a member of the congregation council as set forth in the constitution.

I will be accountable in all my actions to God, self, and the other members of this council and the congregation.

I will uphold all group decisions and not engage in gossip or disrespectful conversation regarding any member of this council or congregation.

I will support the pastor and staff of the congregation as they fulfill their roles of leadership.

reflect, and decide. Once a decision is reached, however, agree to uphold all council actions. Include this stipulation as part of your council covenant. And then hold each other accountable to it.

Council members who engage in public or hidden attacks on group decisions undermine the leadership of the group. They also engage in destructive behavior by acting out a divisive spirit. That's a form of triangulation.

Recognize and avoid triangulation

One council member isn't relating well with the rest of the council, so instead of speaking about her concerns in a council meeting, she seeks an allegiance with another member of the congregation. She complains to this person about the actions the council took last night. She uses indirect communication and unfair techniques to calm her own anxiety.

Triangulation can take many forms in congregations. Individuals, groups, and committees can all be drawn into battles that aren't really about them. Triangulation occurs when someone comes to you to complain about another person or group, or you have a problem with another person and take it to a third party for consultation. It also can happen when a complaint is raised indirectly: "A lot of people are talking and they agree with me that . . ." (You can fill in the blanks with any issue.)

> Congregation councils need to model and encourage direct communications at all times.

Congregation councils need to model and encourage direct communications at all times. If someone comes to you to complain about the pastor, ask if they have spoken directly to the pastor about the concern. Encourage the parties to talk to each other and to discuss all concerns. Don't get caught in the trap of trying to protect someone. Know what your responsibility is and state it clearly. Develop or refer back to your own guidelines for effective communications. (See chapter 5 for more details on creating guidelines for communications.) Do not let those engaging in triangulation dictate the course of your congregation's ministry.

State expectations clearly

For more on job descriptions, see the books **Our Staff: Building Our Human Resources** *and* **Our Structure: Carrying Out the Vision.**

When everyone knows their role or responsibilities in an organization, people are more likely to stay on track and things run more smoothly. For staff members, this can be spelled out in job descriptions. Review job descriptions annually, but not in conjunction with decisions about salary. A job description isn't about money. It's about the boundaries, roles, and expectations that we have for those who are called to serve us.

Consider job or task descriptions for all committees. Let each committee develop its own description for the council to review. This could be done annually or biannually. Look at how everyone interacts as a ministry team. Reviewing the work of the entire ministry structure of the congregation is much healthier than overfocusing on the pastor and paid staff.

Growing Together: Spiritual Exercises for Church Committees also offers opportunities for group prayer, reflection, and sharing.

Publicize your committee job descriptions so that everyone knows who does what. Consider compiling a handbook for congregational leaders that includes committee job descriptions as well as the names and telephone numbers of leaders and committee members. Why not include your council covenant, guidelines for communication, and your congregation's mission statement? This also could be a great handout for new members who want to become familiar with your congregation.

Pray and study together

Amid conflict, remember that as a congregational leader you are but a steward of the church of Jesus Christ. No matter how severe the storms seem, he alone is the one who can quiet the blustering winds and the crashing waves. Seek Christ's peace amid the storm through group prayer and Bible study. When the storm clouds gather, make time for prayer and study when your council or other leadership group meets. It's critical for leaders to be centered and focused on prayer and Bible study during the storms. (Make use of the "African

Bible Study Method" on pages 109-110 in the conflict toolbox. It encourages listening, reflection, and prayer for one another.)

Committees and ministry teams

The Evangelism Committee has now heard about the complaints that the pastor's leadership style and preaching are keeping people away from church. They decide to make recommendations about changing the style of worship back to what it was before this pastor arrived. Maybe if the worship returned to that of the "good old days" then attendance might, too.

Like pastors and councils, committees can fall into the trap of losing their focus and getting caught up in the fray. They can be thrown off track by any of the following:

1. The committee's true purpose and the tasks needed to accomplish that purpose are unclear.
2. No clear boundaries have been established and an overzealous committee may try to do things beyond their realm of responsibility, which causes conflict with other groups.
3. Committees aren't working as part of the ministry team and each has its own goals and mission—or worse yet, none at all. Not working as part of the team does not work well in the body of Christ.

Define roles and expectations

It's important for committee goals, roles, and expectations to be clearly defined and agreed upon by the committee members and the congregation's leadership.

Have each committee create a job or task description. Make sure committee descriptions include the following:

- Accountability (who the committee reports to).
- The committee's purpose or major focus.
- The responsibilities included in fulfilling the stated purpose.
- Who on the committee is responsible for what.

Tasks that do not fulfill the ministry purpose of the committee should be reviewed. Is the wrong committee handling them? Should the Evangelism Committee recommend changes in worship?

Keep communication active

Establish a communications procedure with the council and committees. Is there a council representative on each committee? If not, is there a way for committees to report on their meetings to the council? Committee reports should include all committee actions and any items requiring the action of the council.

Are monthly highlights from the congregation council meeting published in the newsletter? How about committee highlights? Are minutes from meetings posted or otherwise made available to interested members?

Make sure that the channels of communication are kept open so that all hands on deck know who is doing what and when.

Pray together

Open every committee meeting with prayer and devotions.

Open every committee meeting with prayer and devotions. A Bible reading will focus you on the real business of the church.

Committees also can make use of the book *Growing Together: Spiritual Exercises for Church Committees* and the African Bible Study Method tool on pages 109-110.

Conflict will only tear the ship apart if leaders allow that to happen. Strong pastoral and congregational leadership can weather any storm. Just remember who is really in charge of the ship!

Summary

- The pastor, congregation council, and committees must stay focused on their tasks and roles during times of conflict.
- Strong leadership from the pastor is critical during conflict to focus on the healing power of Word and Sacrament.

- Recognize that change will shift the balance of congregational life. There will be an attempt to stabilize and to move backward.
- Ask questions to depersonalize conflict.
- Individuals should be accountable for their own words and actions.
- Focus on building trust and a spirit of cooperation on the congregation council.
- Leaders should pray for one another during conflict. You are in it together.
- Don't forget that it is Jesus who stills the storms around us and in us.

Chapter 7

Storm Cleanup

Following Christ has nothing to do with success
as the world sees it. It has to do with love.

Madeleine L'Engle, *Walking on Water: Reflections on Faith and Art*

The raging winds calm and the convulsing seas settle. The dense clouds break up and you can see the blue sky again. The brunt of the storm has passed, and now it's time to assess damage. It's been a rough and sometimes terrifying ride. The crew is somewhat battered and bruised from being tossed about. The ship itself is in some need of attention and repair. The hull is splintered and supplies below deck have fallen off the shelves. There is much debris on the shore. It's time to clean up after the storm and get things back in order.

After you have endured a tempest, concentrate on healing and recovering a sense of wholeness for both the leaders and the congregation. Start by acknowledging what you've been through and that you have indeed weathered the storm together. This is also a time to thank God for giving you the strength to hold on when all seemed lost. God's love and power to transform you will be your source of healing, too.

Living in the light of forgiveness

The dawn of a new day in your communal life begins when ominous clouds are replaced by the rays of God's forgiveness shining through the words and deeds of your life together.

Spend time in your congregation council, committees, or other working groups talking about the meaning of forgiveness—what it looks like and what it feels like:

- How is forgiveness being expressed in your congregation now? What do you need to work on?
- Has forgiveness been all-embracing or are some people excluded? Are these people on the outside because they do not want reconciliation or because members of the community are reluctant to include them?

You can't force reconciliation on someone who is not ready for it, but you can make sure you are not the one who has built the walls of exclusion.

Use the "Forgiveness Discussion and Liturgy" found on pages 111-112 in the conflict toolbox. Consider holding a congregational healing service or baptismal renewal and forgiveness service to celebrate your passage through the storm. Every passage through a conflict is a form of death and resurrection. How can you recognize this resurrection moment in the life of your congregation? Celebrate the meaning of dying and rising in the waters of baptism. Acknowledge through Word and Sacrament the broken state of humanity and the incredible healing power of God's love.

How can you recognize this resurrection moment in the life of your congregation?

Forgiveness is the foundation of our identity as the people of God. Each of us is like the prodigal son who desperately needed to return to the father and acknowledge his unworthiness and sinfulness. We make mistakes. We go astray. We can't change the past, but we can build our future on the power of God's love to accept us and recreate us.

Moving into the future

Strongly grounded in forgiveness and the recognition that your community is in need of healing, put some concentrated effort into the clean-up efforts so that you can indeed move ahead into the future.

Unhealthy conflict can damage our communications, identity, and vision for ministry. Once you've come through a difficult time, it's important to assess where you are in these areas. Often you'll discover that you've been knocked off course. Are course corrections necessary? Spend time focusing on each of these three areas. This can be done in three basic steps: reconnect, redefine, and redirect.

Reconnect: renewing communications

What were my personal strengths during the conflict?

The first level where you need to reconnect is with yourself as a leader. Conflict usually brings out negative emotions and anxieties in each of us. Now is the time to look for the positive that has occurred as a result of what you've been through. Start by asking yourself what you might have done differently as you negotiated the storm. Don't neglect to ask even more important questions: What were my personal strengths during the conflict? What did I do well? Make a list of your strengths and your gifts. Save it. You'll need it the next time a storm threatens.

Do this with your congregation council or other leadership group, too. During an evening dinner or retreat, focus on reflection and sharing. After the conflict has passed, congregational leaders need to heal and then concentrate on maintaining or rebuilding healthy communications. The agenda might include the following:

1. Dinner or fellowship time for reconnecting.

2. Reflection: How do the individual members of your group interpret your passage through the storm? They might each complete the following sentences.
  • During the conflict, I felt . . .
      Now I feel . . .
  • During the conflict I thought . . .
      Now I think . . .
  • My greatest hope for the congregation is . . .

3. Discussion:
  • Work to identify both your individual strengths and your corporate strengths (as a unified body) in dealing with the conflict as a group and as a congregation. How can your

individual and collective strengths be used as assets on which
to build the future?

- During the conflict, was the communication between your
  group and the congregation effective? If not, where can
  improvements be made?
- Where did you find your peace in the situation? How did you
  seek to ground yourself spiritually in tough times? How have
  you learned more about the presence of God in your life as a
  result of passing through the conflict?

4. End with a celebration of Holy Communion

Share what you have learned with the congregation, perhaps
through a series of newsletter articles or temple talks during worship. Focus on your strength and growth as the people of God.
Keep it honest, but upbeat. Remember that through Jesus Christ
all things are made new. That includes individuals, your group,
and your congregation.

Through Jesus Christ all things are made new. That includes individuals, your group, and your congregation.

The congregation also needs time to reconnect with each other.
Provide opportunities for the congregation to come together,
enjoy each other's company, and have some fun. This is all part of
healing. Gathering for potluck dinners or special theme events,
such as congregational talent shows, can uplift the spirit of the
community.

Redefine: renewing your identity

Every life experience contributes to how we see ourselves and
how we interpret the world around us. During the cleanup after a
storm, redefine who you are as a congregation in light of what
you've been through. How have congregational dynamics been
changed? How can you use your individual and collective
strengths to define who you are now? By reframing what you've
been through in a positive light, you use the experience as a
growth moment, individually and collectively.

Surviving and growing through the storms raises our personal pain thresholds and means that we are indeed stronger than we were. Empowered by the Holy Spirit, we can move forward in a positive direction.

If you and other leaders in your congregation believe that the conflict you have been through has indeed transformed your identity and mission, this might be a time to concretely redefine your congregational mission. The dispute you just endured may really have been the birth pains of a new identity and call to a new direction for serving Christ in your locality.

When we read the book of Acts, we see the early church struggling with an identity crisis. Once their identity changed, so did their mission in the world. They were transformed from a Jewish sect that celebrated the resurrection of Jesus Christ to a missionary church that reached out to Gentiles. They developed an outward focus on witnessing and evangelism. They used their internal conflict and the conflict with the world to fuel their zeal for sharing the gospel.

What new possibilities have now opened up for you? When was the last time you reviewed your congregation's mission statement? This might be a good time to look at the mission statement again.

Redirect: renewing your vision

Where do you go from here?

After you've discussed where you've been, your method of communications, and your identity, the next question is: Where do you go from here? How is your mission defined and supported by your vision?

Your congregation's vision is how you see yourselves actively and concretely living out your mission. It's your dream for the future, your collective goals as the people of God.

Pastors and lay leaders often try to be all things to all people. You need to face the fact that you've just gone through a tough conflict. Because of this, you might feel exhausted and you will need to care for yourself, too. If needed, synods and judicatories might have staff members or other resource people who can come to your congregation and lead workshops on vision discernment.

A solid visioning process includes education and communication. Here are some examples.

- Invite all congregational leaders and members to contribute their ideas.
- Brainstorm dreams or visions of where you'd like the congregation to head in the next three to five years.
- Provide an opportunity to study the Bible to see where God is calling you, as a community in Christ.
- Do a reality check of your local setting. Where are you located? What is the community projected to be in five to 10 years? There is no sense in planning a day-care center for a community that is rapidly aging. Check your local planning board for information on your community.
- Put your dreams, Bible study, and findings about the community in writing. Then provide opportunities for feedback from the congregation. Revise this document as needed and vote on it as a congregation.
- Make a list of what needs to be done to achieve the vision for the congregation.
- Establish a process for review of the progress and relevance of the vision as time goes by. It is always acceptable to adjust your vision over time, to adapt to new situations.

After the storm: self-care for leaders

Much has changed since your congregation has weathered the storm, including you. Don't stop taking time to care for yourself now. During a storm, adrenaline is pumping. Once you're through the storm, you need time for rest, recovery, and spiritual

See the book *Our Mission: Discovering God's Call to Us* for additional information on developing a mission statement and goals for the future.

See *Our Context: Exploring Our Congregation and Community* for more information on examining your setting.

rejuvenation. Take time for yourself after the storm. It's not unusual for illness to strike after navigating through a tough time.

Continue to maintain a focused spiritual discipline through prayer and reading the Bible. Think about creating an entirely new discipline through the use of religious music or focused meditation to invigorate your spiritual life. Where do you feel lacking? What action can you take? Take an extra day off to work on your personal and spiritual needs. Look for a retreat or workshop that might invigorate you. If you feel you need permission to take time for yourself, read the invitation in Mark 6:30-32. How will you respond to Jesus?

Also take time to debrief with synod or judicatory staff or trusted colleagues. Seek to address and resolve your feelings about what transpired in a healthy manner so that you aren't haunted by ghosts of the recent past. Keep the list of your strengths in front of you and accentuate the positive.

Summary

Take the following steps to clean up after the storm:

- Focus on and celebrate God's love and forgiveness for us all.
- Assess the need for corrections in your ministry course.
- Reconnect through renewed communications on three levels: *self*, *leaders*, and *congregation*.
- Redefine and positively reframe who you are as a community of faith as a result of your experience.
- Redirect your vision for your ministry based on your newly perceived strengths.
- Make self-care a continuing priority.

Epilogue

But you are a chosen race, a royal priesthood, a holy nation, God's own people, in order that you may proclaim the mighty acts of him who called you out of darkness into his marvelous light.

Once you were not a people,
 but now you are God's people;
 once you had not received mercy,
 but now you have received mercy.

1 Peter 2:9-10

When we endure through conflicts, we learn that conflict is no fire-breathing dragon waiting to devour us. Conflict can provide an opportunity to live and to grow in our faith and in our relationship with God and each other.

The Bible reads as an identity crisis of the people of God. There is struggle among the people and confusion regarding their direction. There is rebellion against God. We, too, are part of the epic story of God's love.

When we learn to deal with conflict in healthy ways and keep it in the light, we can learn to trust God and grow through all things. Conflict doesn't have to escalate. But even when it does, all is not lost.

Once we come to accept that we will make mistakes and inadvertently hurt each other at times, we can understand the immensity of God's love for us. God fully knows who we are and that we will fall short. Yet God's forgiveness is more powerful than even our greatest shortcomings. God's love and forgiveness is more encompassing than even our greatest conflict.

Let us strive to live as the people of God—in the light, in mercy, and in forgiveness. Let us strive through all things to grow in our relationship with our Creator.

Recommended Resources

Chapter 1: Our Perceptions of Conflict

Edwards, Lloyd. *How We Belong, Fight, and Pray: The MBTI as Key to Congregational Dynamics.* Bethesda, Md.: Alban Institute, 1998. Uses the Myers-Briggs Type Indicator to examine how different personality types view and maneuver through conflict situations.

Leas, Speed B. *Discover Your Conflict Management Style.* Bethesda, Md.: Alban Institute, 1997. Discusses a variety of management styles for dealing with conflict and offers a tool to assess your preferred style.

Chapter 2: Who We Are as People of God

Smith, J. Walker, and Ann Clurman. *Rocking the Ages: The Yankelovich Report on Generational Marketing.* New York: Harper Collins, 1997. Provides a typology of generational differences. The generational time line of historical events is especially useful for discussion.

Strauss, William, and Neil Howe. *Generations: The History of America's Future, 1584 to 2069.* New York: William Morrow, 1991. While the authors' cyclical theory for interpreting history is controversial, the extensive discussion of characteristics of 20th and 21st century generations is useful.

Chapter 3: Family Systems and Congregational Dynamics

Freidman, Edwin H. *Generation to Generation: Family Process in Church and Synagogue.* New York: Guilford Press, 1985. Discusses the interaction and relationship of family systems process to congregational life.

Gilbert, Roberta M. *Extraordinary Relationships: A New Way of Thinking about Human Interactions.* New York: John Wiley & Sons, 1992. Examines themes such as conflict, cut-off, distancing, and how one might move toward healthier personal relationship patterns.

Richardson, Ronald W. *Creating a Healthier Church: Family Systems Theory, Leadership, and Congregational Life.* Minneapolis: Augsburg Fortress, 1996. Applies family systems to the congregation and includes questions for group study and discussion.

Chapter 4: Community Conflict

Halverstadt, Hugh. *Managing Church Conflict*. Louisville, Ky.: Westminster/John Knox Press, 1991.

Johnson, Barry. *Polarity Management: Identifying and Managing Unsolvable Problems*. Amherst, Mass.: HRD Press, 1996. Offers a methodology to deal with unsolvable problems in organizations.

Mayer, Bernard. *The Dynamics of Conflict Resolution: A Practitioner's Guide*. Jossey-Bass, 2000.

Shrock-Shenk, Carolyn, and Lawrence Ressler, eds. *Making Peace with Conflict: Practical Skills for Conflict Transformation*. Herald Press, 1999.

Steinke, Peter. *Healthy Congregations: A Systems Approach*. Bethesda, Md.: Alban Institute, 1996. Uses a systems approach to explain how interpersonal interactions within congregations can contribute to the health or illness of the community.

Steinke, Peter. *How Your Church Family Works*. Bethesda, Md.: Alban Institute, 1996. Discusses how congregations operate as emotional systems.

Chapter 5: Learning Life Skills

Day, Katie. *Difficult Conversations: Taking Risks, Acting with Integrity*. Bethesda, Md.: Alban Institute, 2001. Contains models for communicating about difficult issues.

Hands, Donald R., and Wayne L. Fehr. *Spiritual Wholeness for Clergy: A New Psychology of Intimacy with God, Self and Others*. Bethesda, Md.: Alban Institute, 1994. Provides suggestions for clergy on developing and maintaining healthy relationships and a healthy spirituality.

Pappas, Anthony G. *Pastoral Stress: Sources of Tension/Resources for Transformation*. Bethesda, Md.: Alban Institute, 1996. Examines the various stress factors that enter pastoral life, offering reflection and ideas for transformation for worn-out clergy.

Chapter 6: Surviving the Storms

Cloud, Henry, and John Townsend. *Boundaries: When to Say Yes, When to Say No, To Take Control of Your Life*. Grand Rapids, Mich.: Zondervan, 1992. Looks at several categories of personal boundaries in our lives and discusses when they are healthy and unhealthy.

Hopkins, Nancy Myer, and Mark Laaser, eds. *Restoring the Soul of a Church: Healing Congregations Wounded by Clergy Sexual Misconduct.* Collegeville, Minn.: Liturgical Press, 1995. Contains a collection of essays on issues related to clergy sexual misconduct and all who are affected by this breach of conduct.

Web site: www.ministryhealth.net

Ministry Health: Support and Resources for Pastors and Church Ministry Professionals, Ministry Health LLC, 2930 Hessel Street, Rochester Hills, MI 48307. Examines many issues of ministry, from conflict to clergy health.

Chapter 7: Storm Cleanup

Bandy, Thomas G. *Vision Discernment: The Congregational Workbook.* Port Aransas, Tex.: Easum, Bandy, and Associates, 2000. Also downloadable at www.easumbandy.com. Leads a congregation and its leaders through a process of vision discernment.

Bandy, Thomas G. *Moving Off the Map: A Field Guide to Changing the Congregation.* Nashville: Abingdon Press, 1998. Offers a cutting edge approach to congregational mission transformation.

Melander, Rochelle, and Harold Eppley. *Growing Together: Spiritual Exercises for Church Committees.* Minneapolis: Augsburg Fortress, 1998. Provides devotions for spiritual growth and team building among your leadership groups.

Melander, Rochelle, and Harold Eppley. *The Spiritual Leader's Guide to Self-Care.* Bethesda, Md.: Alban Institute, 2002. Provides 52 exercises for pastors and lay leaders.

Oswald, Roy M. *Clergy Self-Care: Finding a Balance for Effective Ministry.* Bethesda, Md.: Alban Institute, 1998. Addresses the stresses of pastoral ministry and offers assessment and disciplines for self-care.

Parsons, George, and Speed Leas. *Understanding Your Congregation as a System: Congregational Systems Inventory.* Bethesda, Md.: Alban Institute, 1995. Uses several categories and polarities to examine the congregational system currently at work in your congregation.

Chapter 1 Tool

Change, Conflict, and You

Self-Assessment

We experience change on many different fronts, including self, home, work, and congregation. When we undergo intense changes in our own life and health, we will surely be more anxious and on edge. Too much change can overwhelm anyone.

As leaders, what is happening in our lives can have an effect on our congregations. We need to explore the changes in our lives—both positive and negative—and how they affect us. When we understand the impact of change in our lives, we can have a clearer understanding of change and its influence in the congregational system.

List all the changes that are happening in your life and answer the questions for each of the following categories. Under changes for yourself, you might include a change in weight, health, or feelings about your life. Home changes might include a child going off to college or a death in the family. Congregational changes could be a drop in membership, the hiring of a new staff member, or a change to the traditional liturgy.

List changes happening in your life, with yourself:

_____

_____

- Why do you think these changes are happening?
- How did these changes occur? Were the changes anticipated or unanticipated?
- What thoughts and feelings do you have about these changes? Do they cause stress?
- How might you deal with the stress caused by these changes?

List changes happening in your home:

_____

_____

- Why do you think these changes are happening?
- How did these changes occur? Were they anticipated or unanticipated?
- What thoughts and feelings do you have about the changes?
- How might you deal with the stress caused by these changes?

List changes happening in your work:

_____

_____

- Why do you think these changes are happening?
- How did these changes occur? Were they anticipated or unanticipated?
- What feelings do you have about the changes?
- How might you deal with the stress caused by these changes?

List changes happening in your congregation:

_____

_____

- Why do you think these changes are happening?
- How did these changes occur? Were they anticipated or unanticipated?
- What thoughts and feelings do you have about the changes?
- How might you deal with the stress caused by these changes?

Closing thought

Do you find any connections between conflicts that you have experienced personally because of change and conflicts caused by change in your congregation?

Chapter 1 Tool

Hooks and Hot Spots

Self-Assessment

Start by reading Galatians 1:6-24. Paul had a hot spot that caused his anger to rise. What's happening here? Why do you think Paul reacted with such strong language?

We all have hooks and hot spots that have potential to draw us into conflict. Sometimes our temperature rises because something that is happening now reminds us of a problem from the past that we have never healed from. When we are aware of these things, we have better control over them and over our responses.

We all have hooks and hot spots that have potential to draw us into conflict.

1. Read the list of words on page 94. Circle all the words that elicit an emotion in you.

2. Then draw a star next to those words that produce the strongest emotions in you. What emotions do you feel? Do you know why you react that way?

3. Identify your feelings and what triggers them. Strong negative emotions often are rooted in the past. Can you associate a past event with the words that produce negative emotions in you?

4. Think about the way your feelings about past events affect your leadership in the congregation.

How do you react to these words?

Abusive	Gossip
AIDS	Grief
Alcoholic	Hate
Alienation	Holy Communion
Alzheimer's disease	Homosexuality
Ambulance	Hospitalization
Anger	Illness
Anxiety	Insecurity
Baptism	Jesus Christ
Boundaries	Judgmental
Cancer	Laughter
Change	Lies
Church	Love
Combat	Manipulation
Communication	Panic
Conflict	Power
Control	Rape
Counseling	Rejection
Death	Repentance
Deceit	Respect
Denial	Responsibility
Depression	Secrecy
Discrimination	Sex
Domination	Sexism
Drugs	Sorrow
Evil	Suicide
Faith	Trust
Fear	Vision
Fight	Vulnerability
Forgiveness	War
God	Weakness

Chapter 2 Tool

Bible Study on Matthew 18

Group Exercise

Use this tool to study the meaning of forgiveness, repentance, and reconciliation in the body of Christ.

1. Matthew 18 is a directive regarding how we should act as the people of God when there are conflicts and dissension among us. Read the following segments of the chapter and list the central idea of each passage.

   Matthew 18:1-5
   Matthew 18:6-9
   Matthew 18:10-14
   Matthew 18:15-20
   Matthew 18:21-22
   Matthew 18:23-35

2. What progression do you see in these passages? What is their relationship to each other?
3. What do you see as Jesus' central message to us in the whole of Matthew 18?
4. How does your community currently reflect the directive given to us in Matthew 18? Do you exhibit direct communication with one another? Is there a tendency to gossip before approaching an offending party?
5. Are there ways that you can grow in your community life under the directive of Matthew 18? If so, what are they?

Generational Values in Your Congregation

Group Exercise

Begin by reading Genesis 17:1-8. Then pray together:

Lord, we give you thanks for the promise that you gave to Abraham. We thank you also for blessing us with the many generations that come together to worship and praise your name here in our congregation. May we continue to celebrate the diversity of viewpoints and life experiences that we each bring to your church on earth. Empower us to use our individual gifts so that we might serve you and build up your church into the next generation and beyond. Amen

To a large degree, our values are based on the historical context in which we were raised. Our worldview and the values we developed in our youth affect us throughout our lives.

Take time as individuals to answer the following questions. Share your responses and perceptions in the large group. The facilitator for this discussion might refer to *Generations: The History of America's Future, 1584 to 2069*, by Neil Howe and William Strauss (New York: William Morrow, 1991) or visit their Web site at www.fourthturning.com for more information on the characteristics of the generations.

Generation	Birth Years
G.I.	1901–1924
Silent	1925–1942
Boomer	1943–1960
13th generation	1961–1981
Millennial	1982–200?

1. I am a part of the _____ generation.
2. Think of a TV or radio show from your youth. What values were portrayed?
3. What was the pace of life? What was done for leisure?
4. What was the dominant method of mass communication (radio, TV, the Internet, and so on)?
5. What were the dominant views on family when you were 10 years old?
6. What major world events occurred during your youth? How did they influence the future?
7. What was the dominant view of the church during your youth?
8. What were the dominant views on money, work, responsibility, and possessions as you grew up?
9. What values are now held widely by members of your generation?
10. Are any values from different generations in opposition to each other?
11. What have you discovered within your group about the links between generations and values?
12. As people of God, how might we use generational differences as assets rather than as things that divide us?

Chapter 3 Tool

Conflict and Your Family of Origin

Self-Assessment and Group Exercise

Use this tool during a committee or council meeting. Or use it at a council retreat to reflect upon the views of conflict you learned in your family of origin. Reflect individually on the questions first, then share responses in pairs. Finally, share what you have learned with the larger group. This process will take approximately one hour.

Respect personal boundaries during your discussion. No one should be required to speak if they are uncomfortable.

1. Think of several conflicts that occurred within your family while you were growing up. Jot them down.

2. How was conflict viewed in your family of origin?

3. How was conflict handled or resolved? If possible, give an example of a resolution for one of the conflicts you listed above.

4. How does your family of origin's way of dealing with conflict affect you today?

5. Has your method of handling conflict changed as you have matured? If so, how?

6. Within your group, are there any extreme differences in the way conflict was handled in the family of origin or in the way individuals deal with conflict today? If so, what are these differences?

7. How might your differences or similarities in handling conflict affect the dynamics of your group?

Chapter 3 Tool

Personal Concerns and the Congregation

Self-Assessment for Lay Leaders

As leaders, we need to be aware of not only what is happening in the congregation but also what is happening in our lives at the moment. Sometimes we might get overwhelmed with congregational conflicts and carry them home. Other times we might have an argument with a spouse or child and carry that into the congregation. Neither situation is healthy.

1. Take time to reflect on your current personal concerns using the chart on page 100. Concerns would include the challenges of daily life that we struggle hard to either overcome or avoid.

2. At any point have personal concerns affected your leadership in the congregation? If so, how? What might you have done to keep your personal issues at home?

3. Have concerns from the congregation ever affected your personal life? If so, how? What might you have done to change that?

4. On a scale of 1 to 10, with 1 being low and 10 being high, what is your current level of stress and anxiety? How do you feel your current stress level is impacting your effectiveness as a leader in the congregation?

	Major concerns for you
Congregation	
Family Any concerns as a son/daughter, sibling, spouse, parent, grandparent, and so on.	
Finances	
Friends	
Health	
Home	
Leisure activities	
Neighborhood and community	
Work	
World issues	

Chapter 3 Tool

Personal Concerns and the Congregation

Self-Assessment for Pastors

Pastors are at great risk for burnout and self-abuse. We often think that the call to serve God should take priority over everything else, including health and emotional welfare. However, when we are depleted in one area of our life, it begins to show up in others.

1. *Read 1 Timothy 3:1-13.*
- What does Paul list as qualifications for a congregational leader?
- How qualified to serve do you feel at the moment?
- Why does Paul connect congregational leadership and personal life?
- What connections do you see between your home life and your congregational leadership?

2. *Take time to reflect on your current personal concerns.*
- How stressful is your life at the moment? Do you have feelings of being overwhelmed? Are there similar issues in your home life and congregational life?
- How would you rate your current church life? What emotions do you have regarding your church life?
- How would you rate your current personal life? What emotions do you have regarding your personal life?
- Is there balance in your life or are you depleted in some area?

3. *Fill out the chart on page 102.*
- Note major concerns or issues facing you in each area, any ways these concerns impinge upon your work, and possible solutions.

	Major concerns for you	Ways this impinges on your work	Possible solutions
Congregation			
Family Any concerns as a son/daughter, sibling, spouse, parent, grandparent, and so on.			
Finances			
Friends			
Health			
Home			
Leisure activities			
Neighborhood and community			
Work			
World issues			

Chapter 4 Tool

Congregational Conflict Monitor

Group Exercise

Read these two sets of passages on living in the light:
John 8:12-15
1 John 1:5-10

What the leaders of your congregation think and how they want the congregation to change is critical for moving from the darkness into the light. Use this tool to identify the feelings of your congregational leaders about the current status of the congregation.

Ask the group for their ratings on the following items. Use large sheets of paper to chart the average of the responses. Note if there are large variations in the responses. Use a 1-to-5 scale to rate the following: 1 = strongly disagree, and 5 = strongly agree.

1. We have had a high rate of conflict in our congregation.
       1   2   3   4   5

2. There always seems to be conflict in our congregation.
       1   2   3   4   5

3. Our leaders perceive the same amount of conflict within our congregation.
       1   2   3   4   5

4. Our leaders agree on a method to handle conflict within our congregation.

1   2   3   4   5

5. We lost more than five members over the last major congregational conflict.

1   2   3   4   5

6. Over the past five years, we lost more than 10 members over conflict issues.

1   2   3   4   5

7. Over the past five years, we have taken in more members than we have lost.

1   2   3   4   5

8. We are good at resolving our congregational conflicts.

1   2   3   4   5

9. As a congregation, we need to better develop our communication skills.

1   2   3   4   5

10. As Christians, we should be able to live together with fewer conflicts.

1   2   3   4   5

11. Our congregational conflicts focus on the same themes and issues.

1   2   3   4   5

12. Our leaders maintain support of group decisions once decisions are made.

            1   2   3   4   5

13. We tend to deny conflict when it exists in our congregation.

            1   2   3   4   5

14. It embarrasses me that disagreements occur in our congregation.

            1   2   3   4   5

15. When we seek the guidance of the Holy Spirit, we can work out our differences.

            1   2   3   4   5

Discussion

Your ratings on these items indicate how you perceive conflict in your congregation. These ratings also suggest what your leadership group and congregation can work on.

- What do you see as areas for improvement? (Do you need to deal with how to handle conflict? Is there a need for better communications?)
- What would you need to feel more empowered to deal with conflict? If you learn to break past dysfunctional patterns, change can begin to occur.

Conflict usually is a faith issue at the root: Are we trusting God? Are we trusting others? Are we trying to overpower God and others? If we do trust in God, we can resolve conflicts and learn to live in the light.

Chapter 5 Tool

Defining Self in Community

Group Exercise

Most people have been so ingrained in their style of communicating that they may not recognize it as being unfair at times. This exercise could be used as part of a council retreat or general meeting to identify unfair communication techniques and teach fair techniques.

Our communications are more effective and honest when we speak for ourselves and state our opinion. People may not agree with us, but at least they will know what we think. The more we define ourselves in our conversation, the less likely we are to use unfair communication techniques by speaking for others or unfairly pulling in third parties to back us.

1. Review the following statements. Which statements define self? Put a check in the "S" column for self-defining.

2. Statements that are not self-defining often seek to control or define others. Which statements seek to define others? Put a check in the "O" column for others. What do you suppose is the intent behind the "O" statements? What other guidelines for fair communications are being broken with the "O" statements?

3. Rewrite the "O" statements to make them more self-defining and fair.

Sample "S" statement: It's just my opinion, but I think we should canvass the community at Christmas and Easter to try and attract new members.

Sample "O" statement: Pastor, you didn't visit my father when he was in the hospital, and he's very upset.

S   O

_____ _____   1. Pastor, you didn't visit my father when he was in the hospital, and he's very upset.

_____ _____   2. It's just my opinion, but I think we should canvass the community at Christmas and Easter to try and attract new members.

_____ _____   3. Several of us have discussed the hymns we've sung these past few weeks, and we want easier hymns that the congregation can actually sing.

_____ _____   4. Rumor has it that the congregation council wants to buy that vacant lot next to the church and build an addition. Don't you think we should do something about it before they get too far?

_____ _____   5. Nobody wants to change the way we do communion. We're all used to it this way.

_____ _____   6. I believe that worship is the central thing that we do as a church. It's where I come to be fed each week.

_____ _____   7. I love to hear the children's choir sing in church. They add such vitality to the service.

_____ _____   8. I can run this committee any way I see fit!

_____ _____   9. If we could only change the attitude of certain people in this congregation we wouldn't have any trouble. Maybe they should start listening to the sermon each week!

S   O

____   ____   10. We can't have youth dressed like that in church! Whatever happened to the days of respect for God and dressing up for church?

____   ____   11. When I was in the church office, I happened to notice an anonymous note on the secretary's desk complaining about the length of today's service. So, what are you going to do about it?

____   ____   12. The shut-ins are upset since they haven't been visited in months. I called around to check on some of them and they were all complaining.

____   ____   13. While I know there may be some debate, I think it's time to consider adding a contemporary service to our schedule.

____   ____   14. You just don't understand the members of this church the way that I do!

____   ____   15. I disagree with letting that group use our church hall each week.

____   ____   16. Oh, that's just the way she always reacts to things. We just ignore her around here.

Chapter 6 Tool

African Bible Study Method

Group Exercise

The African Bible Study Method, also called "Lambeth," focuses on meditative study and letting the passage speak to you on an emotional level. There is no discussion of the sharing, just acceptance and reflection.

The following passages might be helpful for those dealing with conflicted situations:

Matthew 18:15-20	Church discipline
Mark 4:35-41	Jesus stills the storm
Luke 6:27-36	Love your enemies
Luke 12:1-3	Secrets uncovered
Luke 15:1-7	The lost sheep
John 13:31-35	The commandment to love
John 14:15-17, 25-27	The coming of the Spirit
Romans 12:1-8	Transformation in Christ
1 Corinthians 1:26-31	Boast only in Christ
2 Corinthians 4:1-7	The power is God's
Colossians 3:12-17	Live in Jesus' name
James 1:19-27	Do God's word

Select a Bible passage for group study and meditation and use the following format.

1. *Read the passage out loud.*
- Reflection: Identify the word or phrase with which you connect. What touches you?
- Share your word or phrase with the group.

2. *Read the passage out loud again.*
- Reflection: How does this passage connect with your life today?
- Share your reflection with the group.

3. *Read the passage out loud again.*
- Reflection: How is God inviting me to change in what I've heard or shared?
- Share your reflection with the group.

4. *Join hands for a circle prayer.*

Each person prays for the one on his or her right and that person's shared learnings or concerns.

The African Bible Study Method was used by the African Delegation to the Lambeth Conference of the Anglican Church in 1996.

Chapter 7 Tool

Forgiveness Discussion and Liturgy

Group Exercise

Note to leader: Seat your group in a circle for this exercise.

Discussion

Read the following verses aloud:
- Matthew 18:21-22
- Luke 6:37-38
- Luke 23:34

Take time to reflect on and discuss the following:
- What do the biblical texts tell us about forgiveness?
- What does forgiveness mean to you?
- How do you know when someone forgives you? What are the signs?
- How do you go about forgiving someone for a wrong done to you?
- Does it make a difference to you if the wrong was done intentionally or unintentionally?
- How can we strive to make forgiveness a way of life? What steps might we take, personally and as leaders?

Confession

All take hands around the circle.

Leader: God of Grace, our days are filled with many things, including the need to forgive those who have wronged us and the need to be forgiven by others for injuries that we have committed-—both intentionally and unintentionally. We ask that you would fill us with your Spirit so that our desire for personal repentance is pure and true. We ask that you also fill us with a desire to live a life of grace toward those around us so that we might more freely express forgiveness to those who hurt us. In Jesus' name. Amen

I ask all gathered around this circle of fellowship, do you earnestly ask God to forgive you the wrongs that you have committed?

People: With a penitent heart, I ask God to forgive my wrongs, both intentional and unintentional.

Absolution

Bow your heads and close your eyes for a moment of silent prayer.

The leader squeezes the hand of a person next to him or her. Then that person looks up and the leader pronounces the words of forgiveness: "Jesus forgives you and so do I." The leader will bow his or her head and the newly forgiven person will repeat the act to their neighbor, then bow his or her head. Go around the circle in this manner. When you are finished going around the circle, take time for silent group reflection.

Leader: God of grace and mercy, we thank you for the love you have for each one of your children which lights our way even when we are lost and confused. Empower us with your Holy Spirit so that we may follow your example and strive to live lives of daily grace and forgiveness—in the name of the Father, and of the Son, and of the Holy Spirit. Amen